Dedication

To my stepfather, Guy A. Olson, August 27, 1927 – June 20, 2003.
Guy always encouraged me and he signed on the dotted line when it meant
the most for me. I thank him for everything. He is missed.

Acknowledgments

I want to thank my husband and children for all your patience while I was working on this book. I couldn't have done it without your support.

Thanks to my family and friends who wondered where I'd disappeared to but didn't give up on me—especially my mom, Janice Olson. Thank you.

I would also like to thank the staff at my shop for their encouragement, their hard work, their friendly smiles, and the nice firm kicks they gave me when I needed them: Manette Lamping, Kay Murphy, Cindy Pederson, Vickie Zobel, and Danielle Gerstner.

I especially want to THANK (in capital letters!!!) Mary Anderson, my quilter on staff, for getting the projects quilted "like yesterday" when I needed them.

Thank you, Grandma, for teaching me to love fabric and creativity when I was still a little girl.

And thank you, Martingale & Company, for the opportunity to realize a dream.

D1378475

Contents

Introduction

THE MAIN project for this book is a block-of-the-month quilt I designed for the customers at my shop, The Quilted Forest, in Forest City, Iowa. It appeared in a small local newspaper and the instructions were also available in the shop. Halfway through the year I thought to myself, "This would make a great book! I could add a variety of individual projects based on each of the blocks and include lots of fun ideas!" And that's just what I did.

The book is divided into 12 monthly lessons. Each lesson includes instructions for making one or more blocks for the main project, "Seeing Stars Quilt." In a couple of instances, the monthly addition isn't really a block (it's actually a unit or strip), but for the sake of consistency, I'm calling it a block. Month 12 includes instructions for putting all of the blocks together to make the quilt.

Included with the monthly lessons are great individual quilt projects that feature the lesson blocks. There is a wide range of project sizes and types, and in many cases a different lesson block of the same size could be substituted for the one featured.

Because of the way I make my triangle squares, there is often a smaller finished triangle square left over after I stitch and trim the triangle square for the project. Some of the monthly lessons include instructions for a bonus project made with these leftover triangle squares from the individual project. Note that bonus projects are basically an idea for what you can do with the leftover triangle squares and they do not include a materials list. (I recommend using graph paper to draft the design first and once that's established, determine how much fabric you'll need for the project.) I include other ideas for using these leftover triangle squares on page 93.

How to Use This Book

THERE ARE lots of ways the block-of-the-month idea can be used. First, you can decide to make the main quilt on your own. Work on one block each month, every other week, each week, or whatever time frame you need to finish the quilt. By only working on a small portion of the quilt at a time, it won't be such an overwhelming project.

Small groups of friends can use the book and the main quilt as the basis for a round-robin project. In a round-robin, each participant purchases a copy of the book and makes the first block using fabrics of their own choosing. They then pass the block to another member of the group, who makes the second block from the book, incorporating her own fabrics. The blocks are passed on to each member of the group until each member has made at least one block for each of the other members. The blocks are returned to the person who made the first block. It is more fun if participants keep the blocks secret from each other, agreeing that they won't see their finished blocks again until the end when the blocks are done. A quilting retreat at the end of the year would be an excellent opportunity to present the blocks to each other, sew the blocks together, and spend quality time as a group.

The main quilt would also make a great project for a group to work on as a fund-raising quilt. Each member of the team could make blocks from one or more of the monthly lessons. Group members would get together to combine their blocks and piece the quilt top together. The quilt could be hand quilted by the group or machine quilted by a qualified machine quilter, and finished off with a binding and label party.

You might also want to consider using the quilt for a raffle, a Habitat for Humanity house, a charity auction, or as a special gift to someone in need.

These are just ideas to get you started on your way to making a very special quilt from a very special book. Enjoy!

General Instructions

IF YOU'RE just starting to quilt or need to brush up on your skills, this chapter will take you through the basics of what you need to know to make the quilt top. For finishing instructions, refer to "Finishing Techniques," beginning on page 89.

Fabric

I GOT a little carried away and made the main project "Seeing Stars Quilt," in four different color schemes: patriotic, batik, black-and-white, and brights. As you can see, it really doesn't matter what colors you use. Just be sure to select fabrics with plenty of variety in color, scale, and texture. A quilt with a wide variety of these elements will be interesting to look at and to create.

Let's start with color. In the patriotic quilt, I used red, white, and blue. Within the reds are different tones of reds: some lighter, some darker, some bright, and some muted. The same is true for

"Seeing Stars Quilt" in patriotic colors

"Seeing Stars Quilt" in batiks

the blues. Some are navy, some royal, and some a deep, dark blue. In the black-and-white quilt, I used several shades of black and even threw in some gray for additional "color." The result is stunning. For the bright quilt, I found that bright fabrics were fun to pick. My fabric criteria for that quilt was, "Does it knock my socks off?" If it did, I included it!

Scale is the next factor you should consider when selecting prints. Include a variety of small prints, medium prints, and larger allover prints. Don't forget to add a few solids or fabrics that read as solids so that the eye has a place to rest.

Dots, checks, plaids, vines, floral designs, swirls, and any repeated design determine a fabric's texture. A variety of these will always keep the viewer interested.

When selecting the fabrics for your project, lay them on a table or attach them to a design wall and stand back 6' to 10' if you can to determine which of the fabrics to include. Ask yourself the following questions to help you decide if these fabrics are the right ones for the project:

- Do all the fabrics appear to be the same? (If they do, there isn't enough variety!)
- Do I have enough diversity in color?
- Are there different scales represented in the prints?
- Is there an assortment of textures?
- Are there any fabrics that stand out and will bother me if I put them in the quilt?

Do not overthink this process. Go with your first instincts, play a little, and make a quick decision. It is only a quilt after all! Making the blocks should take longer than choosing the fabrics. If selecting fabrics is difficult for you, get help at a

"Seeing Stars Quilt" in black and white

"Seeing Stars Quilt" in bright colors

local quilt shop or from a friend whose quilts you admire for their color choices.

Buy the highest-quality fabrics you can afford. The old adage "You get what you pay for" applies to fabric, too. Fabrics at quilt shops are usually a higher quality than those available at discount stores. The dyes and finishes are better, the fabrics are softer, and they have been printed on better-quality goods than their counterparts.

Should you prewash your fabrics? This is a personal decision and every quilter is entitled to his or her own opinion. I do not wash my fabrics before I put them in a quilt. Here's why: I like the way fabric feels as it comes off the bolts, I use only high-quality fabrics from reputable companies because they are less likely to bleed and fade with time, and I am usually too anxious to start a project to wait for fabric to come out of the washer, then the dryer, and then be pressed. Plus, fabrics that are washed after they're pieced and quilted tend to shrink into the batting just a bit, giving the quilt an amazing well-loved and cozy look.

If I am concerned about a particular fabric's dye wandering onto its neighbor, I do test the fabric. My test involves soaking a test square of the fabric in some warm water and laying it on a white paper towel. If it will be a problem fabric, dye will migrate to the paper towel almost immediately. At this point I can choose to treat the offending fabric with a dye fixative or just get another fabric.

There are times when I do recommend prewashing fabrics—when working with heirloom quilts that are to be hand quilted, when using fabrics from an unknown source (such as old fabric from an estate sale), or when the quilter or intended recipient has allergies to the chemicals used to treat fabrics. For those occasions, it is necessary to wash the fabric to prevent problems above and beyond dye migration!

Finally, the yardage requirements for the quilts in this book are based on fabric that is at least 42" wide. If your fabric is narrower than 42", you may need to purchase additional yardage.

Thread

JUST LIKE fabric, you should use a high-quality, 100%-cotton thread when machine piecing. Your local quilt shop should have a couple of brands from which to choose. Do not scrimp on thread! Many tension and thread-breakage problems are because of inferior thread or very old thread. Do not use old thread your grandmother gave you or that you purchased at an antique store!

When choosing a thread color for machine piecing, pick one that is neutral to the project. What is neutral for one project won't work for all projects. I tend to sew with a soft pink color for both bobbin and top threads when working on lighter fabrics. Surprisingly, pink blends well into many of the lighter, pastel, and white fabrics. A soft brown or dark tan works great with darker colors. Pick out your thread when you are selecting your fabrics. You may think you have it at home, and some of you might, but it's better to be safe than sorry. I don't know how many times I've come home with materials for a project and not had the right thread color when I thought I did.

Hand quilters will need to purchase hand-quilting thread to use for the quilting process. Hand-quilting thread has a special coating on it to help it glide through the fabric layers. Gliding thread through beeswax or a product called Thread Heaven will also help the thread go through the fabric easier and make nasty knots a thing of the past. Hand quilters should also try to use a thread that blends in with most of the fabrics. If they want their quilting to stand out and get noticed, they will need to use a contrasting color.

Machine quilters can have a little fun with their quilting threads. I mostly use and recommend 100%-cotton threads for machine quilting. They are the same fiber content as the fabric you make your quilts out of and will be the gentlest on your fabrics. However, I also love to play with different thread types and colors for machine quilting. Variegated threads are fun to use and leave a subtle pattern within the quilting. Rayon threads add some extra shine and shimmer. Polyester threads are strong, easy to quilt with, and sometimes, depending on the manufacturer, come in a wider array of colors than their cotton counterparts. There really is no limit to what you can use for machine quilting.

Once you select your thread for machine quilting, you'll also want to determine what color to use. The best way to do this is to lay the quilt top on a table near a light source. Drape about three to six yards of thread over the quilt top in a random fashion. I will usually try four or five colors at once. Try some threads just for the fun of it, even if you don't think they will work. Often those are the threads that will surprise you and be the perfect match. Sometimes, the one that you think will work will be the only one that doesn't! Look at your choices up close and from a distance of 5' to 10'. Sometimes it takes a while to find the right thread and just as often, you find it on the first try. The point here is this: Try many and sew with one. Unless, of course, you want to quilt with more than one thread color! Some quilts just need it.

There is just one type of thread that I refrain from using: monofilament thread. I worry about the effect this strong thread will have on my quilt and on the metal parts in my sewing machine. I usually do not recommend this thread or use it myself. However, many people like to use this thread because it is invisible and they don't have to pick a color. They often use it sparingly on smaller wall hangings and items that won't get a lot of rough use.

Rotary Cutting

ALL OF the pieces used to make the projects in this book were cut with a rotary cutter. I can hardly imagine quilting without using a rotary cutter, self-healing mat, and an acrylic ruler. Learning to use a rotary cutter isn't difficult and takes just a little practice to perfect. Being accurate with your cuts is very important. If you are off by as little as ⅛", it will be difficult for your blocks to measure to the proper size when finished.

The first step in rotary cutting is to straighten one edge of your fabric. Fold the fabric in half lengthwise and align the selvages. Lay the fabric on the cutting mat with the fold closest to you. Place a long see-through ruler on the right-hand side of the fabric so that the edge of the ruler completely covers both layers of fabric. Align a horizontal line of the ruler with the fold of the fabric. Cut along the right edge of the ruler, through both layers of fabric. Now you are ready to cut strips.

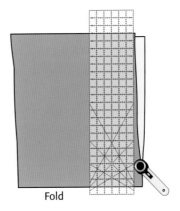

Fold

Rotate the fabric so that the newly cut edge is on your left. It is best to do this without moving the fabric, so either rotate your mat or move to the opposite side of the cutting surface. Place the vertical line of the ruler that corresponds to the strip width on the straightened edge of the fabric. Cut along the right edge of the ruler. If you are cutting a lot of strips from the same fabric, open the strips occasionally to make sure they are still straight. If you find that they have developed a bend, re-straighten the edge.

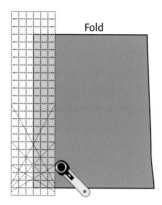
Fold

Once you have cut the strips, you are ready to cut squares and rectangles from them. Place the folded strip on the cutting surface with the selvages to the right. Remove the selvages and straighten the ends of the folded strip by aligning a horizontal line of the ruler with the long edge of the folded strip; cut along the right edge of the ruler as before when you straightened the yardage. Rotate the strip so that the cut edge is on the left. Align the proper measurement on your ruler with the straightened end of the strip; cut.

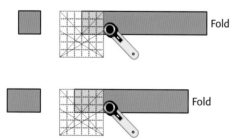
Fold
Fold

Seam Allowances

Use a ¼" seam allowance for all seams unless indicated otherwise. It is very important for seams to be accurate. If your seam allowance is greater than ¼", by even just two thread widths, over the course of eight seams in a block you could subtract up to a ½" from the correct measurement of a block! A seam allowance that is less than ¼" will cause blocks to measure larger than they should. Either way, sashings, alternate blocks, or borders will not work with the blocks. Test your ¼" seam allowance by sewing two 1" x 4" rectangles together. This unit should measure 1½" wide all the way across. Keep testing your seam until you get it right! You won't regret it.

STAY SHARP

When was the last time you changed the needle in your sewing machine or the blade in your rotary cutter?

For best results, it is recommended that you change the needle in your machine at the beginning of every project or after 8 to 16 hours of sewing. The time will vary with the project or type of fabric you are working with, so you may need to change it more often.

Changing the blade on your rotary cutter will certainly improve your enthusiasm for cutting! It is much easier to control the cutter if the blade is sharp and free of nicks. Also, the blade will roll easier if the screw holding it isn't as tight as it can be. When you set the cutter on your mat and roll it forward, the blade should roll freely. If it doesn't, gradually loosen the screw until it does.

Double Star Block

FINISHED BLOCK SIZE: 16" x 16"

Materials

Yardages are based on 42"-wide fabrics.

- ⅜ yard of light-colored fabric (B) for outer-star background and center square
- ¼ yard of a different light-colored fabric (A) for inner-star background
- ¼ yard of dark-colored fabric (C) for inner-star points
- ¼ yard of a different dark-colored fabric (D) for outer-star points

Cutting

All measurements include ¼"-wide seam allowances.

From light-colored fabric A, cut:
- 4 squares, 2½" x 2½"
- 4 rectangles, 2½" x 4½"

From light-colored fabric B, cut:
- 5 squares, 4½" x 4½"
- 4 rectangles, 4½" x 8½"

From the inner-star point fabric (C), cut:
- 8 squares, 2½" x 2½"

From the outer-star point fabric (D), cut:
- 8 squares, 4½" x 4½"

Piecing the Block

1. Use a sharp pencil or fabric marking pen to draw a diagonal line from corner to corner on the wrong side of the C and D squares.

2. Place a C square on one end of an A rectangle as shown, right sides together. Stitch on the marked line. Stitch again, ½" from the first stitching line as shown. Cut between the two lines. Set aside the trimmed corner. Press the seam toward the dark fabric. Repeat on the other end of the rectangle, positioning the square as shown, to complete an inner-star-point unit. Make four.

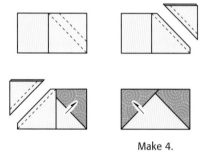

Make 4.

3. Sew an inner-star-point unit to the top and bottom of a B square as shown. Press the seams toward the square. Sew an A square to the ends of the remaining inner-star-point units. Press the seams toward the squares. Sew these units to the sides of the B-square unit to make the inner-star unit. Press the seams in the

directions indicated. The square should measure 8½" x 8½".

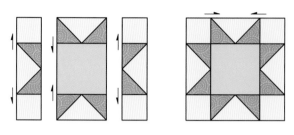

4. Refer to step 2 to use the B rectangles and the D squares to make the star-point units for the outer star. Make four.

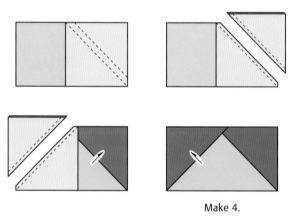

Make 4.

5. Refer to step 3 to sew the outer-star-point units and the remaining B squares to the inner-star unit to finish the block. The block should measure 16½" x 16½".

Friendship Star Blocks

NOTE: *You will be making four of these blocks every month (except months eight and twelve) using the fabric left over from that month's fabric requirements. The blocks will be used to make the inner border of the main quilt. These blocks are scrappy and they do not all need to look exactly alike. Make some blocks with light stars on a dark background and some with dark stars on a light background. You could even have some dark stars on a dark background! There are no wrong fabric choices.*

Cutting

All measurements include ¼-wide seam allowances. The cutting requirements are for 1 block. Cut pieces from the desired fabrics to make 4 blocks.

From 1 fabric (A), cut:
* 8 squares, 2½" x 2½"

From the other fabric (B), cut:
* 5 squares, 2½" x 2½"

Piecing the Blocks

1. Place an A and B square right sides together. Use a sharp pencil or fabric marking pen to draw a line from corner to corner on the wrong side of the lighter square. Stitch on the marked line. Stitch again, ½" from the first stitching line as shown. Cut between the two lines. Set aside the trimmed corner (see "Spare Triangle Square Ideas" on page 93). Press the seam toward the darker fabric. Make four.

Make 4.

2. Arrange the triangle-square units and the remaining A and B squares into three horizontal rows as shown. Stitch the pieces in each row together. Press the seams toward the plain squares. Stitch the rows together to finish the block. The block should measure 6½" x 6½".

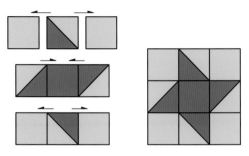

3. Make a total of four Friendship Star blocks from the leftover fabrics.

TIME AND FABRIC SAVER

If making the extra triangle squares doesn't interest you, use your favorite method for making triangle squares. The finished triangle squares should measure 2" (2½" before being sewn into a block). There are plenty of products on the market to make these. For example, the 6" Bias Square® ruler, the ScrapMaster® ruler, the Easy Angle ruler, Triangles-on-a-Roll papers, and Thangles all offer optional methods for making triangle squares. This may be a good time to try several of the methods and decide which one is your favorite!

Double Star Baby Quilt

FINISHED QUILT SIZE: 40" x 58½"

Materials

Yardages are based on 42"-wide fabrics.

- 1½ yards of multicolored print fabric for outer-star background and inner-star center square
- 1⅛ yards of dark pink fabric for sashing, border, and binding
- ⅞ yard of lime green fabric for outer-star points
- ½ yard of white fabric for inner-star background
- ⅜ yard of light pink fabric for inner-star points
- 2½ yards of fabric for backing
- 46" x 65" piece of batting

Cutting

All cutting measurements include ¼"-wide seam allowances.

From the light pink fabric, cut:

◆ 3 strips, 2½" x 42"; crosscut the strips into 48 squares, 2½" x 2½"

From the lime green fabric, cut:

◆ 6 strips, 4½" x 42"; crosscut the strips into 48 squares, 4½" x 4½"

From the white fabric, cut:

◆ 5 strips, 2½" x 42"; crosscut the strips into:
  - 24 rectangles, 2½" x 4½"
  - 24 squares, 2½" x 2½"

From the multicolored print fabric, cut:

◆ 10 strips, 4½" x 42"; crosscut the strips into:
  - 30 squares, 4½" x 4½"
  - 24 rectangles, 4½" x 8½"

From the dark pink fabric, cut:

◆ 9 strips, 3" x 42"; crosscut 6 strips into:
  - 3 strips, 3" x 16½"
  - 4 strips, 3" x 35"
◆ 6 strips, 2½" x 42"

Piecing the Blocks

1. Use a sharp pencil or fabric marking pen to draw a diagonal line from corner to corner on the wrong side of each light pink and lime green square.

2. Place a light pink square on one end of a white rectangle as shown, right sides together. Stitch on the marked line. Stitch again, ½" from the first stitching line as shown. Cut between the two lines. Set aside the trimmed corner for use in "Pinwheel Piggies Baby Quilt," the bonus project on page 20, or for use in another project (refer to "Spare Triangle Square Ideas" on page 93). Press the seam toward the pink fabric. Repeat on the other end of the rectangle,

positioning the square as shown, to complete an inner-star-point unit. Make 24.

Make 24.

3. Sew an inner-star-point unit to the top and bottom of a multicolored print square as shown. Press the seams toward the square. Sew a white square to the ends of two inner-star-point units as shown. Press the seams toward the squares. Sew these units to the sides of the multicolored print square to make an inner-star unit. Press the seams in the directions indicated. Make six inner-star units. The squares should measure 8½" x 8½".

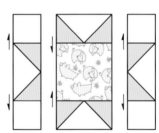

Make 6.

4. Refer to step 2 to use the lime green squares and the multicolored print rectangles to make the star-point units for the outer star. Make 24.

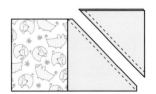
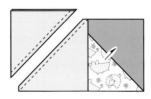
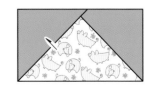
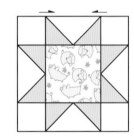

Make 24.

5. Refer to step 3 to sew the outer-star-point units and the remaining multicolored print squares to the inner-star units to finish the blocks. Make six Double Star blocks. The blocks should measure 16½" x 16½".

Make 6.

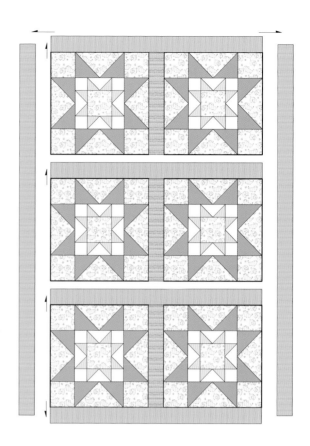

Assembling the Quilt Top

1. Refer to the quilt assembly diagram to sew a Double Star block to each side of a dark pink 3" x 16½" strip to make a block row. Press the seams toward the dark pink strips. Make three rows.

2. Sew a dark pink 3" x 35" strip to the top of each block row. Sew the rows together. Add the remaining dark pink 3" x 35" strip to the bottom of the quilt top. Press the seams toward the dark pink strips.

3. Join the dark pink 3" x 42" strips end to end to make one long strip. Refer to "Adding Borders" on page 89 to measure the quilt top for the side borders. From the pieced strip, cut two side border strips to the length measured. Sew the strips to the sides of the quilt top. Press the seams toward the borders.

Finishing the Quilt

Refer to "Finishing Techniques" on page 89.

1. Piece the quilt backing so that it is approximately 6" longer and 6" wider than the quilt top.

2. Layer the quilt top, batting, and backing; baste the layers together.

3. Quilt as desired. This quilt was machine quilted with an allover quilting pattern of stippling and hearts. Hand quilting in the ditch, around the stars, and the sashing would also be very effective and simple.

4. Bind the quilt with the dark pink 2½"-wide strips.

5. Add a label to the back of your project.

Pinwheel Piggies Baby Quilt

1. Press open all the spare triangle squares you saved from "Double Star Baby Quilt." You should have 48 *each* of the large and small triangle squares. You will use all of the large triangle squares and all but eight of the small triangle squares for this quilt. Set those aside for another project.

2. Measure the large triangle squares and trim them all to the size of the smallest one. Repeat with the small triangle squares.

3. Sew four large triangle squares together as shown to make a large Pinwheel block. Make 12. Repeat to make 10 small Pinwheel blocks using the small triangle squares.

Make 12.   Make 10.

4. Cut 17 sashing strips. These pieces should be as wide as the small Pinwheel blocks and as long as the large Pinwheel blocks.

5. Sew three large blocks and two sashing strips together as shown to make the block rows. Make four. Sew three sashing strips and two small blocks together as shown to make the sashing rows. Make three.

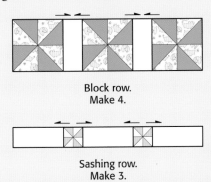

Block row.
Make 4.

Sashing row.
Make 3.

6. Refer to the quilt assembly diagram to sew the block rows and sashing rows together as shown.

7. Measure the quilt-top sides and top and bottom for border strips. Cut the border strips the width of the small Pinwheel blocks (unfinished size), and the quilt-top lengths just measured, piecing as necessary.

8. Sew the inner side borders to the sides of the quilt top. Press the seams toward the border strips. Sew a small Pinwheel block to the ends of the top and bottom border strips. Add these strips to the top and bottom of the quilt top. Press the seams toward the border strips.

9. Refer to "Adding Borders" on page 89 to measure the quilt for the outer top and bottom border strips. Cut the border strips to the desired width and the length measured, piecing as necessary. Sew the strips to the top and bottom of the quilt top. Press the seams toward the border strips.

10. Measure the quilt top for the outer side border strips. Cut the strips the same width as the outer top and bottom border strips and the length measured, piecing as necessary. Sew the strips to the sides of the quilt top. Press the seams toward the border strips.

11. Refer to "Finishing Techniques" on page 89 to layer the quilt top, batting, and backing; baste the layers together. Quilt as desired and bind the quilt edges. Add a label to the back of the quilt.

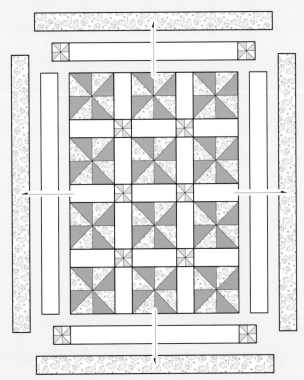

Rail Units and Friendship Star Blocks

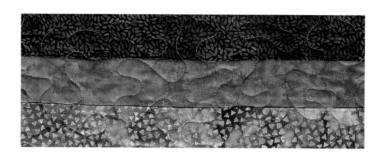

FINISHED RAIL-UNIT SIZE: 6" x 16"
FINISHED FRIENDSHIP STAR BLOCK SIZE: 6" x 6"

Materials

Yardages are based on 42"-wide fabrics. Materials listed are enough for 4 rail units and 4 Friendship Star blocks.

- ¾ yard of light-colored fabric
- ⅜ yard of dark-colored fabric
- ¼ yard of medium-dark or dark-colored fabric

Cutting

All measurements include ¼"-wide seam allowances.

From the light-colored fabric, cut:
- 8 strips, 2½" x 42"; crosscut 6 of the strips into:
  - 32 squares, 2½" x 2½"
  - 2 strips, 2½" x 28½"
  - 2 strips, 2½" x 32½"

From the medium-dark or dark-colored fabric, cut:
- 2 strips, 2½" x 42"

From the dark-colored fabric, cut:
- 4 strips, 2½" x 42"; crosscut 2 of the strips into 20 squares, 2½" x 2½"

Piecing the Rail Units and Friendship Star Blocks

1. Refer to "Friendship Star Blocks" on page 15 to use the 2½" light and dark squares to make four Friendship Star blocks. These will be stitched to the ends of the rail units and not used in the border.

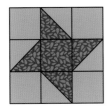

Make 4.

2. Sew a light, medium-dark or dark, and dark 2½" x 42" strip together as shown to make a strip set. Make two. Press the seams away from the light fabric. From the strip sets, cut four segments, 16½" wide.

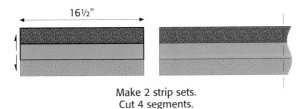

16½"

Make 2 strip sets.
Cut 4 segments.

3. Sew a rail unit to opposite sides of the Double Star block from month one (see page 13). Press the seams toward the rail unit.

4. Sew a Friendship Star block to the ends of each of the remaining rail units. Press the seams toward the rail units. Sew the rail units to the top and bottom of the unit from step 3 to make the center block. The center block should measure 28½" x 28½".

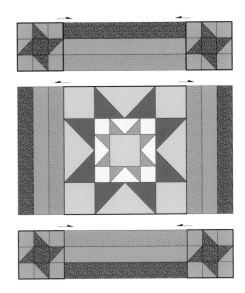

5. Sew the light-colored 2½" x 28½" strips to the sides of the center block. Press the seams toward the strips. Sew the light-colored 2½" x 32½" strips to the top and bottom of the center block. Press the seams toward the strips. The center block should now measure 32½" x 32½".

6. Refer to "Friendship Star Blocks" on page 15 to make four Friendship Star blocks from the leftover fabrics. You should now have a total of eight Friendship Star blocks for the border.

Rails Table Runner

FINISHED TABLE RUNNER SIZE: 19½" x 51½"

Materials

- ⅝ yard of medium blue fabric for rail units and binding
- ⅝ yard of multicolored print fabric for border
- ⅜ yard of white fabric for rail units and Friendship Star blocks
- ⅜ yard of dark blue fabric for rail units and Friendship Star blocks
- 1⅝ yards of fabric for backing
- 24" x 56" piece of batting

Cutting

From the white fabric, cut:
- 4 strips, 2½" x 42"; crosscut 2 strips into 32 squares, 2½" x 2½"

From the dark blue fabric, cut:
- 4 strips, 2½" x 42"; crosscut 2 strips into 20 squares, 2½" x 2½"

From the medium blue fabric, cut:
- 6 strips, 2½" x 42"

From the multicolored print fabric, cut:
- 4 strips, 4" x 42"

Piecing the Blocks and Rail Units

1. Refer to "Friendship Star Blocks" on page 15 to use the 2½" white and dark blue squares to make four Friendship Star blocks.

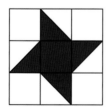

Make 4.

2. Sew a white, medium blue, and dark blue 2½" x 42" strip together as shown to make a strip set. Make two. Press the seams away from the white strips. From the strip sets, cut four segments, 16½" wide.

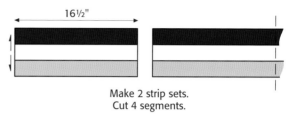

16½"

Make 2 strip sets.
Cut 4 segments.

Assembling the Table Runner Top

1. Sew a Friendship Star block to one end of a rail unit as shown. Make four. Be sure the rail units are facing the same direction, with the dark blue on top. Press the seams toward the rail units. Each unit should measure 6½" x 22½".

Make 4.

2. Sew the units together as shown. Press the seams toward the rail units. The runner top should now measure 12½" x 44½".

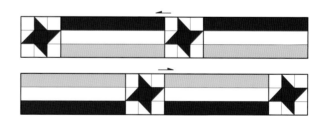

3. Sew three of the multicolored print 4" x 42" strips together end to end to make one long strip. Refer to "Adding Borders" on page 89 to measure the table runner for top and bottom borders. From the pieced strip, cut two strips to the length measured. Sew the strips to the top and bottom edges of the table runner top. Press the seams toward the strips. Measure the table runner top for the side borders. From the

remaining multicolored 4" x 42" strip, cut two strips to the length measured. Sew the strips to the sides of the table runner top. Press the seams toward the strips.

Finishing the Table Runner

Refer to "Finishing Techniques" on page 89.

1. Piece the table runner backing so that it is approximately 4" longer and 4" wider than the quilt top.

2. Layer the table runner top, batting, and backing; baste the layers together.

3. Quilt as desired. This table runner was machine quilted in the ditch of the rail units, and free-motion quilted with a small stipple design on the white rails and the star backgrounds. A large stipple design was used to quilt the border area.

4. Bind the table runner with the remaining medium blue 2½"-wide strips.

5. Add a label to the back of your project.

DOUBLE DUTY

My friends often marvel at all the sewing and reading I'm able to accomplish. What's my secret? Books on CD! While I'm doing repetitive work like sewing strip sets or triangle squares together, I rely on a CD to keep my mind engaged and happy. Pressing hundreds of seams will fly by when you are at the good part in a book! Often I sew much longer than I'd planned because I just couldn't stop "reading." Check out your favorite bookstore or library to see what is available.

Chain Star Blocks

FINISHED BLOCK SIZE: 12" x 12"

Materials

Yardages are based on 42"-wide fabrics. Materials listed are enough to make 8 blocks.

- 1 yard of light-colored fabric
- ⅝ yard of dark-colored 1 fabric
- ⅜ yard of dark-colored 2 fabric
- ⅜ yard of a light or medium accent fabric

Cutting

All measurements include ¼"-wide seam allowances.

From the light-colored fabric, cut:

- 4 strips, 4½" x 42"; crosscut the strips into 32 squares, 4½" x 4½"
- 4 strips, 2½" x 42"

From the dark-colored 1 fabric, cut:

- 4 strips, 4½" x 42"; crosscut the strips into 32 squares, 4½" x 4½"

From the dark-colored 2 fabric, cut:

- 3 strips, 2½" x 42"

From the accent fabric, cut:

- 3 strips, 2½" x 42"

Piecing the Blocks

1. Use a sharp pencil or fabric marking pen to draw a diagonal line from corner to corner on the wrong side of each light-colored square.

2. Place a light-colored and dark-colored 1 square right sides together with the light square on top. Stitch on the marked line. Stitch again, ½" from the first stitching line. Cut between the

two lines. Set aside the trimmed corner (see "Spare Triangle Square Ideas" on page 93). Press the seam toward the dark fabric. Make 32.

Make 32.

3. Sew a light-colored strip to a dark-colored 2 strip to make a strip set. Press the seam toward the dark strip. Make two. From the strip sets, cut 32 segments, 2½" wide.

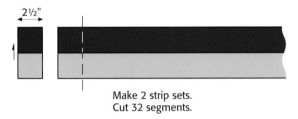

Make 2 strip sets.
Cut 32 segments.

4. Sew two segments from step 3 together as shown to make a four-patch unit. Make 16. The four-patch units should measure 4½" x 4½".

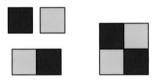

Make 16.

5. Repeat steps 3 and 4 to make two strip sets from the light-colored and accent strips. Press the seam toward the accent strip. Crosscut the strip sets into 32 segments, 2½" wide, and make 16 four-patch units.

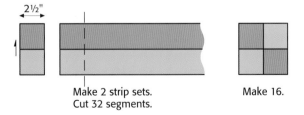

Make 2 strip sets.   Make 16.
Cut 32 segments.

6. Repeat steps 3 and 4 to make one strip set from the remaining accent and dark-colored 2 strips. Press the seam toward the dark strip.

Crosscut the strip set into 16 segments, 2½" wide, and make eight of the four-patch units.

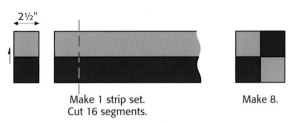

Make 1 strip set.   Make 8.
Cut 16 segments.

DON'T PANIC!

If you can't cut enough segments from your strip sets to make all 16 four-patch units, use 2½" squares of the appropriate fabrics to piece the four-patch units. Sometimes, due to differences in cutting techniques, widths of fabrics, or rotary-cutter operator error, there just aren't enough cuts out of one strip set. Instead of making another whole strip set, it is easier to cut squares and make the four-patch units the old-fashioned way: four squares at a time.

7. Sew the triangle-square and four-patch units into three horizontal rows as shown. Sew the units in each row together. Press the seams toward the triangle-square units. Make eight. The blocks should measure 12½" x 12½".

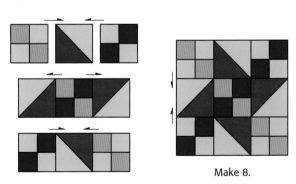

Make 8.

8. Refer to "Friendship Star Blocks" on page 15 to make four Friendship Star blocks from the leftover fabrics. You should now have a nice little stack of 12 blocks.

Chain of Stars Twin-Size Quilt

FINISHED QUILT SIZE: 72½" x 96½"

Materials

Yardages are based on 42"-wide fabrics.

- 5⅛ yards of tan fabric for block backgrounds
- 4 yards of dark red fabric for block triangle-square units and binding

- 2⅞ yards *total* of assorted medium and dark fabrics for block four-patch units
- 6 yards of fabric for backing
- 79" x 102" piece of batting

Cutting

All measurements include ¼"-wide seam allowances.

From the tan fabric, cut:
- 24 strips, 4½" x 42"; crosscut the strips into 192 squares, 4½" x 4½"
- 24 strips, 2½" x 42"

From the dark red fabric, cut:
- 24 strips, 4½" x 42"; crosscut the strips into 192 squares, 4½" x 4½"
- 9 strips, 2½" x 42"

From the assorted medium and dark fabrics, cut a *total* of:
- 36 strips, 2½" x 42"

Piecing the Blocks

1. Use a sharp pencil or fabric marking pen to draw a diagonal line from corner to corner on the wrong side of each tan square.

2. Place a tan and dark red square right sides together with the tan square on top. Stitch on the marked line. Stitch again, ½" from the first stitching line as shown. Cut between the two lines. Set aside the trimmed corner for use in "Love Letters Lap Quilt," the bonus project on page 32, or for use in another project (refer to "Spare Triangle Square Ideas" on page 93). Press the seam toward the dark red fabric. Make 192.

Make 192.

3. Sew a tan strip to a medium or dark strip to make a strip set. Press the seam toward the medium or dark strip. Make 24. From the strip sets, cut 384 segments, 2½" wide.

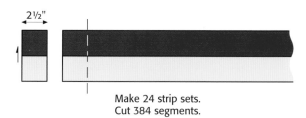

Make 24 strip sets.
Cut 384 segments.

4. Sew two different segments from step 3 together as shown to make a four-patch unit. Make 192. The four-patch units should measure 4½" x 4½".

Make 192.

5. Repeat steps 3 and 4 to make six strip sets from the remaining medium and dark strips. Press the seams toward the darker fabric. Crosscut the strip sets into 96 segments, 2½" wide, and make 48 four-patch units.

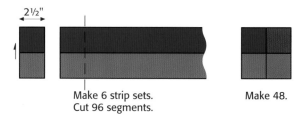

Make 6 strip sets.   Make 48.
Cut 96 segments.

6. Arrange the triangle-square units and the four-patch units into three horizontal rows as shown. Sew the units in each row together, and then sew the rows together to complete the block. Make 48. The blocks should measure 12½" x 12½".

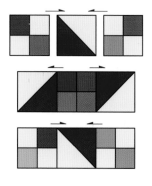
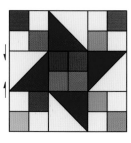

Make 48.

Assembling the Quilt Top

1. Refer to the quilt assembly diagram to arrange the blocks into eight horizontal rows of six blocks each.

2. Sew the blocks in each row together. Press the seams in opposite directions from row to row. Sew the rows together. Press the seams in one direction.

Finishing the Quilt

Refer to "Finishing Techniques" on page 89.

1. Piece the quilt backing so that it is approximately 6" longer and 6" wider than the quilt top.

2. Layer the quilt top, batting, and backing; baste the layers together.

3. Quilt as desired. This quilt was machine quilted in an allover pattern.

4. Bind the quilt with the dark red 2½"-wide strips.

5. Add a label to the back of your project.

USE UP THOSE LEFTOVERS!

I keep bins in my sewing room to hold strips left over from projects. One bin holds 1"-wide strips, another bin holds 1½"-wide strips, and so on up to strips measuring 5" wide. These precut strips come in handy for scrappy quilts, testing blocks, and projects like this one! All of the chain pieces in my quilt were made from leftover binding strips or pieces cut from other quilting projects. It was great to use up stash fabric for this portion of the quilt. And best of all, they were already cut!

Love Letters Lap Quilt

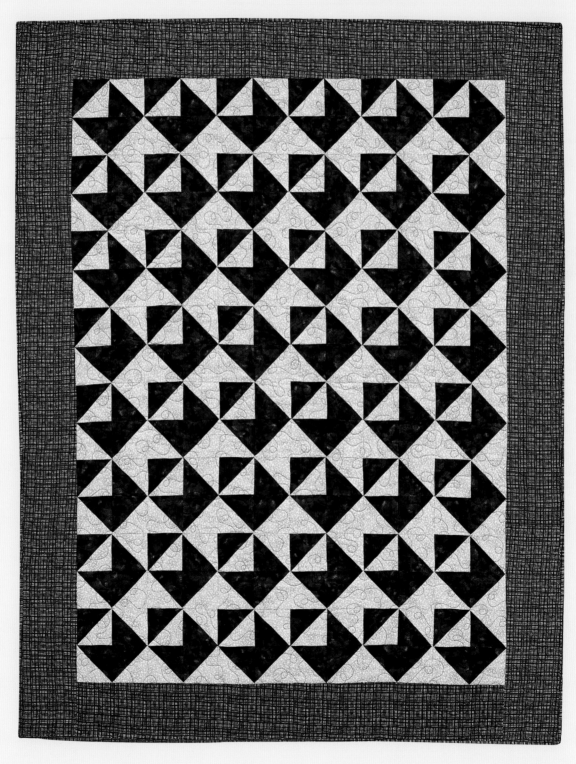

1. Press open all of the spare triangle squares you saved from "Chain of Stars Twin-Size Quilt." You should have 192.

2. Measure the triangle squares and trim them all to the size of the smallest one.

3. Arrange four triangle squares as shown to make the Love Letters block. Make 48.

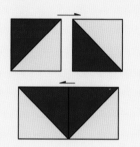 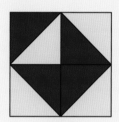

Make 48.

4. Refer to the quilt assembly diagram to arrange the blocks into eight rows of six blocks each as shown. Sew the blocks in each row together. Press the seams in alternate directions from row to row. Sew the rows together. Press the seams in one direction.

5. Refer to "Adding Borders" on page 89 to measure the quilt top for the top and bottom border strips. Cut the border strips to the desired width and the length measured, piecing as necessary. Sew the strips to the top and bottom edges of the quilt top. Press the seams toward the border strips.

6. Measure the quilt top for the side border strips. Cut the strips the same width as the top and bottom border strip and the length measured, piecing as necessary. Sew the strips to the sides of the quilt top. Press the seams toward the border strips.

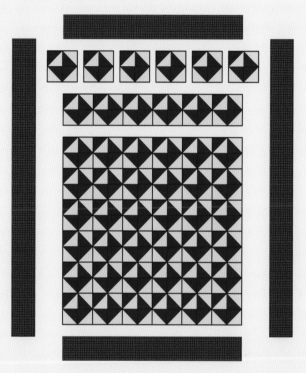

7. Refer to "Finishing Techniques" on page 89 to layer the quilt top, batting, and backing; baste the layers together. Quilt as desired and bind the quilt edges. Add a label to the back of the quilt.

Evening Star Blocks

FINISHED BLOCK SIZE: 12" x 12"

Materials

Yardages are based on 42"-wide fabrics. Materials listed are enough to make 4 blocks.

- ¾ yard of light-colored fabric
- ½ yard of dark-colored fabric
- ½ yard of medium-colored or accent fabric

BABY BIAS EDGES

Be gentle when working with the cut edges of the triangles. They are on the bias grain and will stretch out of shape if not handled carefully. Press gently for the same reason.

Cutting

From the light-colored fabric, cut:

- 4 squares, 5¼" x 5¼"; cut each square in half twice diagonally to yield 16 triangles
- 16 squares, 2⅞" x 2⅞"; cut each square in half once diagonally to yield 32 triangles
- 32 squares, 2½" x 2½"
- 4 squares, 4½" x 4½"

From the medium-colored or accent fabric, cut:

- 4 squares, 5¼" x 5¼"; cut each square in half twice diagonally to yield 16 triangles
- 16 squares, 2⅞" x 2⅞"; cut each square in half once diagonally to yield 32 triangles

From the dark-colored fabric, cut:

- 8 squares, 5¼" x 5¼"; cut each square in half twice diagonally to yield 32 triangles

Piecing the Blocks

1. Sew a large medium-colored or accent triangle to each large light-colored and dark-colored triangle as shown to make a pieced triangle. Press the seams toward the medium-colored fabric. Trim the dog-ears. Make 16 of each combination.

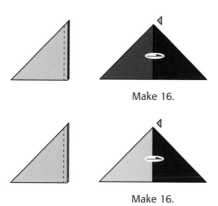

Make 16.

Make 16.

2. Sew one pieced triangle of each combination together as shown to make a quarter-square-triangle unit. Make 16. Press the seam toward the unit with the dark triangle. The units should measure 4½" x 4½".

Make 16.

3. Sew a small light-colored triangle to a small medium-colored or accent triangle to make a triangle square. Make 32. Press the seams toward the medium or accent fabric. Trim the dog-ears. The triangle squares should measure 2½" x 2½".

Make 32.

4. Sew a light-colored 2½" square to each of the triangle squares from step 3 as shown. Make sure all the units are exactly alike. Press the seams toward the light squares.

5. Join two units from step 4 as shown to make the block corner squares. Make 16. The squares should measure 4½" x 4½".

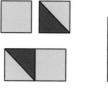

Make 16.

6. Arrange four quarter-square-triangle units from step 2, four corner squares, and one light-colored 4½" square into three horizontal rows as shown. Sew the squares in each row together. Press the seams toward the quarter-square-triangle units. Sew the rows together to complete the block. Make four. The blocks should measure 12½" x 12½".

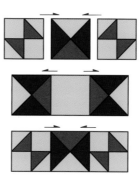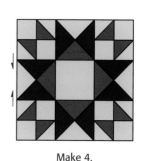

Make 4.

7. Refer to "Friendship Star Blocks" on page 15 to make four Friendship Star blocks from the leftover fabric. You should now have 16 blocks for the border.

Evening Blues Crib Quilt

FINISHED QUILT SIZE: 45½" x 57½"
FINISHED BLOCK SIZE: 12" x 12"

Materials

Yardages are based on 42"-wide fabrics.

- 2 yards of light blue fabric for block backgrounds
- 1½ yards of medium blue fabric for block centers, small star points, and border
- 1⅛ yards of dark blue fabric for large star points and binding
- 3 yards of fabric for backing
- 51" x 63" piece of batting

Cutting

All measurements include ¼"-wide seam allowances.

From the light blue fabric, cut:

- 4 strips, 5¼" x 42"; crosscut the strips into 24 squares, 5¼" x 5¼". Cut each square in half twice diagonally to yield 96 triangles.
- 4 strips, 2⅞" x 42"; crosscut the strips into 48 squares, 2⅞" x 2⅞". Cut each square in half once diagonally to yield 96 triangles.
- 6 strips, 2½" x 42"; crosscut the strips into 96 squares, 2½" x 2½"

From the dark blue fabric, cut:

- 4 strips, 5¼" x 42"; crosscut the strips into 24 squares, 5¼" x 5¼". Cut each square in half twice diagonally to yield 96 triangles.
- 6 strips, 2½" x 42"

From the medium blue fabric, cut:

- 2 strips, 4½" x 42"; crosscut the strips into 12 squares, 4½" x 4½"
- 4 strips, 2⅞" x 42"; crosscut the strips into 48 squares, 2⅞" x 2⅞". Cut each square in half once diagonally to yield 96 triangles.
- 6 strips, 5" x 42"

Piecing the Blocks

1. Sew each large light blue triangle to a dark blue triangle as shown to make a pieced triangle. Make 96. Press the seams toward the dark blue fabric. Trim the dog-ears.

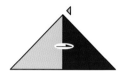

Make 96.

2. Sew two pieced triangles together as shown to make a quarter-square-triangle unit. Make 48. Press the seams in one direction. The units should measure 4½" x 4½".

Make 48.

> **BABY BIAS EDGES**
> Be gentle when working with the cut edges of the triangles. They are on the bias grain and will stretch out of shape if not handled carefully. Press gently for the same reason.

3. Sew a small light blue triangle to each medium blue triangle to make a triangle square. Make 96. Press the seams toward the medium blue fabric. Trim the dog-ears. The squares should measure 2½" x 2½".

Make 96.

4. Sew a light blue 2½" square to each of the triangle squares from step 3 as shown. Make sure all the units are exactly alike. Press the seams toward the light blue squares.

5. Join two units from step 4 as shown to make the block corner squares. Make 48. The squares should measure 4½" x 4½".

Make 48.

6. Arrange four quarter-square-triangle units from step 2, four corner squares, and one medium blue 4½" square into three horizontal rows as shown. Sew the squares in each row together. Press the seams toward the quarter-square-triangle units. Sew the rows together to complete the block. Make 12. The blocks should measure 12½" x 12½".

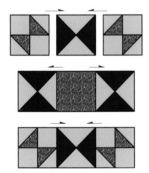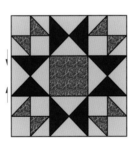

Make 12.

Assembling the Quilt Top

1. Refer to the quilt assembly diagram to arrange the blocks into four horizontal rows of three blocks each.

2. Sew the blocks in each row together. Press the seams in opposite directions from row to row. Sew the rows together. Press the seams in one direction.

3. Refer to "Adding Borders" on page 89 to measure the quilt top for the top and bottom borders. From the medium blue 5" x 42" strips, cut two strips to the length measured. Sew the strips to the top and bottom edges of the quilt top. Press the seams toward the border strips. Join the remaining medium blue strips together end to end to make one long strip. Measure the quilt top for the side borders. From the pieced strip, cut two strips to the length measured. Sew the strips to the sides of the quilt top. Press the seams toward the border strips.

Finishing the Quilt

Refer to "Finishing Techniques" on page 89.

1. Piece the quilt backing so that it is approximately 6" longer and 6" wider than the quilt top.

2. Layer the quilt top, batting, and backing; baste the layers together.

3. Quilt as desired. This quilt was quilted with an allover meandering pattern and light blue thread.

4. Bind the quilt with the dark blue 2½"-wide strips.

5. Add a label to the back of your project.

Spacey Star Blocks

FINISHED BLOCK SIZE: 12" x 8"

Materials

Yardages are based on 42"-wide fabrics. Materials listed are enough to make 4 blocks.

- ½ yard of light-colored fabric
- ⅜ yard of dark-colored fabric

Cutting

All measurements include ¼"-wide seam allowances.

From the light-colored fabric, cut:
- 4 strips, 2½" x 42"; crosscut the strips into:
  - 8 rectangles, 2½" x 10½"
  - 8 rectangles, 2½" x 4½"
  - 16 squares, 2½" x 2½"
  - 4 squares, 4½" x 4½"

From the dark-colored fabric, cut:
- 3 strips, 2½" x 42"; crosscut the strips into:
  - 8 rectangles, 2½" x 4½"
  - 24 squares, 2½" x 2½"

Piecing the Blocks

1. Use a sharp pencil or fabric marking pen to draw a diagonal line from corner to corner on the wrong side of each light and dark 2½" square.

2. Place a dark square on one corner of a light 4½" square as shown, right sides together. Stitch on the marked line. Stitch again, ½" from the first stitching line as shown. Cut between the two lines. Set aside the trimmed corner (see "Spare Triangle Square Ideas" on page 93). Press the seam toward the dark fabric. Repeat on the opposite corner of the square. Make four center squares. The squares should measure 4½" x 4½".

Make 4.

3. Place a dark square on one end of a light 2½" x 4½" rectangle as shown, right sides together. Refer to step 2 to stitch, trim, and press the square. Make eight.

Make 8.

4. Place a light 2½" square on one end of a dark 2½" x 4½" rectangle as shown, right sides together. Refer to step 2 to stitch, trim, and press the square. Make eight.

Make 8.

5. Stitch the pieced rectangles from steps 3 and 4 together as shown. Make eight. Press the seams toward the light rectangle. The squares should measure 4½" x 4½".

Make 8.

6. Sew a square from step 5 to each side of a center square from step 2 as shown. Make four center-row units. The units should measure 4½" x 12½".

Make 4.

7. Place a dark 2½" square on one end of a light 2½" x 10½" rectangle as shown. Refer to step 2 to stitch, trim, and press the square. Sew a light 2½" square to the end of the pieced rectangle as shown. Make eight top/bottom row units.

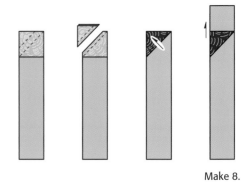

Make 8.

8. Arrange one center-row unit and two top/bottom row units into three horizontal rows as shown. Sew the rows together. Make four. Press the seams toward the top and bottom rows. The blocks should measure 12½" x 8½".

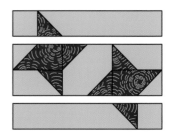

Make 4.

9. Refer to "Friendship Star Blocks" on page 15 to make four Friendship Star blocks from the leftover fabrics. You should now have 20 blocks for the border.

Patriotic Table Runner

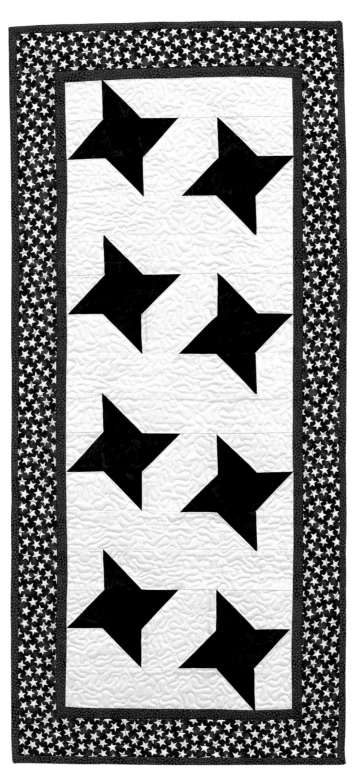

FINISHED QUILT SIZE: 19½" x 39½"
FINISHED BLOCK SIZE: 12" x 8"

Materials

Yardages are based on 42"-wide fabrics.

- ½ yard of white fabric for block backgrounds
- ½ yard of red fabric for inner border and binding
- ½ yard of navy blue print for outer border
- ⅜ yard of navy blue solid for block stars
- 1½ yards of fabric for backing
- 24" x 44" piece of batting

Cutting

From the white fabric, cut:

- 4 strips, 2½" x 42"; crosscut the strips into:
  - 8 rectangles, 2½" x 10½"
  - 8 rectangles, 2½" x 4½"
  - 16 squares, 2½" x 2½"
  - 4 squares, 4½" x 4½"

From the navy blue solid, cut:

- 3 strips, 2½" x 42"; crosscut the strips into:
  - 8 rectangles, 2½" x 4½"
  - 24 squares, 2½" x 2½"

From the red fabric, cut:

- 3 strips, 1" x 42"
- 4 strips, 2½" x 42"

From the navy blue print, cut:

- 3 strips, 3½" x 42"

Piecing the Blocks

1. Use a sharp pencil or fabric marking pen to draw a diagonal line from corner to corner on the wrong side of each white and navy blue solid 2½" square.

2. Place a navy blue square on one corner of a white 4½" square as shown, right sides together. Stitch on the marked line. Stitch again, ½" from the first stitching line as shown. Cut between the two lines. Set aside the trimmed corner (see "Spare Triangle Square Ideas" on page 93). Press the seam toward the navy blue fabric. Repeat on the opposite corner of the square. Make four center squares. The squares should measure 4½" x 4½".

Make 4.

3. Place a navy blue square on one end of a white 2½" x 4½" rectangle as shown, right sides together. Refer to step 2 to stitch, trim, and press the square. Make eight.

Make 8.

4. Place a white 2½" square on one end of a navy blue 2½" x 4½" rectangle as shown, right sides together. Refer to step 2 to stitch, trim, and press the square. Make eight.

Make 8.

5. Stitch the pieced rectangles from steps 3 and 4 together as shown. Make eight. Press the seams toward the light rectangle. The squares should measure 4½" x 4½".

Make 8.

6. Sew a square from step 5 to each side of a center square from step 2 as shown. Make four center-row units. The units should measure 4½" x 12½".

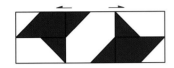

Make 4.

7. Place a navy blue 2½" square on one end of a white 2½" x 10½" rectangle as shown. Refer to step 2 to stitch, trim, and press the square. Sew a white 2½" square to the end of the pieced rectangle as shown. Make eight top/bottom row units.

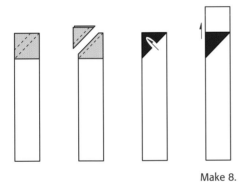

Make 8.

8. Arrange one center-row unit and two top/bottom row units into three horizontal rows as shown. Sew the rows together. Make four. Press the seams toward the top and bottom rows. The blocks should measure 12½" x 8½".

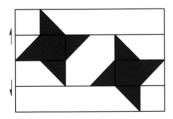

Make 4.

Assembling the Table Runner Top

1. Refer to the table runner assembly diagram to sew the blocks together side by side along the long edges as shown.

2. Refer to "Adding Borders" on page 89 to measure the table runner top for the top and bottom borders. From the red 1" x 42" strips, cut two strips to the length measured. Sew the strips to the top and bottom edges of the table runner top. Press the seams toward the border strips. Measure the table runner top for the side borders. From the remaining strip, cut two strips to the length measured. Sew the strips to the sides of the table runner top. Press the seams toward the border strips. Repeat to add the navy blue print 3½" x 42" strips to the table runner top for the outer border.

Finishing the Table Runner

Refer to "Finishing Techniques" on page 89.

1. Cut the table runner backing so that it is approximately 4" longer and 4" wider than the table runner top.

2. Layer the table runner top, batting, and backing; baste the layers together.

3. Quilt as desired. For this table runner, the white areas feature stippling with white thread, which makes the blue stars stand out. The borders were quilted in the ditch with red thread. A meandering design was used in the outer border.

4. Bind the quilt with the red 2½"-wide strips.

5. Add a label to the back of your project.

Mosaic Star Blocks

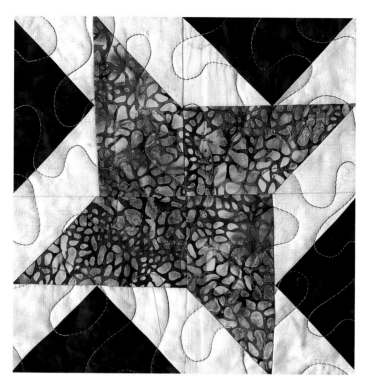

FINISHED BLOCK SIZE: 10" x 10"

Materials

Yardages are based on 42"-wide fabrics.

- ½ yard of light-colored fabric for background
- ½ yard of accent fabric for star
- ⅜ yard of dark-colored fabric for flying-geese units

Cutting

All measurements include ¼"-wide seam allowances. Materials listed are enough to make 4 blocks.

From the light-colored fabric, cut:

- 4 strips, 3" x 42"; crosscut the strips into 48 squares, 3" x 3"

From the accent fabric, cut:

- 3 strips, 3" x 42"; crosscut the strips into 16 rectangles, 3" x 5½"

From the dark-colored fabric, cut:

- 3 strips, 3" x 42"; crosscut the strips into 16 rectangles, 3" x 5½"

Piecing the Blocks

1. Use a sharp pencil or fabric marking pen to draw a diagonal line from corner to corner on the wrong side of the light squares.

2. Place a light square on one end of an accent rectangle as shown, right sides together. Stitch on the marked line. Stitch again, ½" from the first stitching line as shown. Cut between the two lines. Set aside the trimmed corner (see "Spare Triangle Square Ideas" on page 93). Press the seam toward the accent fabric. Make 16.

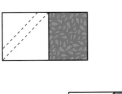

Make 16.

3. Place a light square on one end of a dark rectangle as shown, right sides together. Refer to step 2 to stitch and trim the square. Press the seam toward the dark fabric. Repeat on the other end of the rectangle, positioning the square as shown. Make 16 flying-geese units.

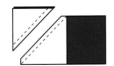

Make 16.

4. Stitch one unit each from steps 2 and 3 together as shown. Press the seam toward the step 2 unit. Make 16. The units should measure 5½" x 5½".

Make 16.

5. Arrange four units from step 4 into two horizontal rows as shown. Sew the units in each row together. Press the seams in the directions indicated. Sew the rows together to complete the block. Make four. The blocks should measure 10½" x 10½".

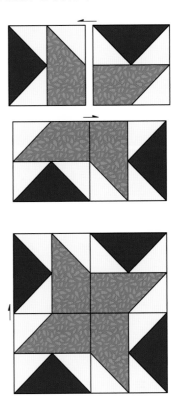

Make 4.

6. Refer to "Friendship Star Blocks" on page 15 to make four Friendship Star blocks from the leftover fabrics. You should now have 24 blocks for the border.

Mosaic Madness Lap Quilt

FINISHED QUILT SIZE: 66½" x 86½"
FINISHED BLOCK SIZE: 10" x 10"

Materials

Yardages are based on 42"-wide fabrics.

- ♦ 4⅛ yards of cream batik for background
- ♦ 4 yards of dark red batik for pinwheels, border, and binding
- ♦ 2⅝ yards of gold batik for stars
- ♦ 5¼ yards of fabric for backing
- ♦ 73" x 93" piece of batting

GENEROUS? CRAZY? OR BOTH?!

This may seem like too much fabric for a quilt this size. It is! Using the method given will create spare triangle squares and use more fabric than if you were to cut the pieces in a traditional manner. However, when you are done with this quilt, you will have a nice-size pile of triangle squares to use for another project!

Cutting

All measurements include ¼"-wide seam allowances.

From the cream batik, cut:

- 45 strips, 3" x 42"; crosscut the strips into 576 squares, 3" x 3"

From the gold batik, cut:

- 28 strips, 3" x 42"; crosscut the strips into 192 rectangles, 3" x 5½"

From the dark red batik, cut:

- 28 strips, 3" x 42"; crosscut the strips into 192 rectangles, 3" x 5½"
- 8 strips, 3½" x 42"
- 8 strips, 2½" x 42"

ONE STEP AT A TIME

Don't let the large number of pieces in this quilt frighten you. I worked on one row at a time to prevent feeling overwhelmed by the project. The results were worth all of the time I put into it. Break the project down into manageable sections to help yourself get through it. This would be a great quilt to work on with a group of friends. You could divide all the spare triangle squares among the group and challenge each other to make something with them!

Piecing the Blocks

1. Use a sharp pencil or fabric marking pen to draw a diagonal line from corner to corner on the wrong side of the cream squares.

2. Place a cream square on one end of a gold rectangle as shown, right sides together. Stitch on the marked line. Stitch again, ½" from the first stitching line as shown. Cut between the two lines. Set aside the trimmed corner (see "Spare Triangle Square Ideas" on page 93). Press the seam toward the cream fabric. Make 192.

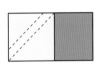
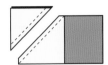

Make 192.

3. Place a cream square on one end of a dark red rectangle as shown, right sides together. Refer to step 2 to stitch and trim the square. Press the seam toward the cream fabric. Repeat on the other end of the rectangle, positioning the square as shown. Make 192.

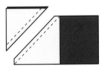

Make 192.

4. Stitch one unit each from steps 2 and 3 together as shown. Press the seam toward the step 2 unit. Make 192. The units should measure 5½" x 5½".

Make 192.

5. Arrange four units from step 4 into two horizontal rows as shown. Sew the units in each row together. Press the seams in the directions indicated. Sew the rows together to complete the block. Make 48. The blocks should measure 10½" x 10½".

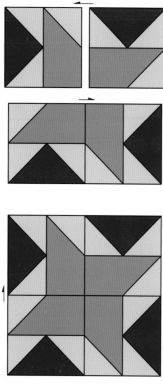

Make 48.

Assembling the Quilt Top

1. Refer to the quilt assembly diagram to arrange the blocks into eight horizontal rows of six blocks each.

2. Sew the blocks in each row together. Press the seams in alternate directions from row to row. Sew the rows together. Press the seams in one direction.

3. Join the dark red 3½" x 42" strips together end to end to make one long strip. Refer to "Adding Borders" on page 89 to measure the quilt top for the top and bottom borders. From the pieced strip, cut two strips to the length measured. Sew the strips to the top and

bottom edges of the quilt top. Press the seams toward the border strips. Measure the quilt top for the side borders. From the remainder of the pieced strip, cut two strips to the length measured. Sew the strips to the sides of the quilt top. Press the seams toward the border strips.

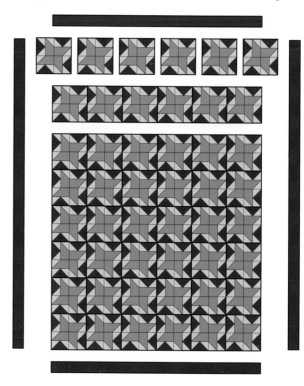

Finishing the Quilt

Refer to "Finishing Techniques" on page 89.

1. Piece the quilt backing so that it is approximately 6" longer and 6" wider than the quilt top.

2. Layer the quilt top, batting, and backing; baste the layers together.

3. Quilt as desired. This quilt was quilted on a long-arm quilting machine with a funky, random quilting design and dark red thread.

4. Bind the quilt with the dark red 2½"-wide strips.

5. Add a label to the back of your project.

Geese in the Stars Block

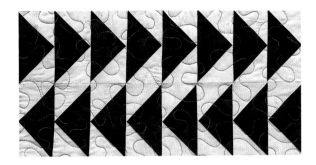

FINISHED BLOCK SIZE: 20" x 10"

Materials

Yardages are based on 42"-wide fabrics.

- ⅜ yard of light-colored fabric
- ⅜ yard of dark-colored fabric

Cutting

All measurements include ¼"-wide seam allowances.

From the light-colored fabric, cut:

- 3 strips, 3" x 42"; crosscut the strips into 32 squares, 3" x 3"

From the dark-colored fabric, cut:

- 3 strips, 3" x 42"; crosscut the strips into 16 rectangles, 3" x 5½"

Piecing the Block

1. Use a sharp pencil or fabric marking pen to draw a diagonal line from corner to corner on the wrong side of the light squares.

2. Place a light square on one end of a dark rectangle as shown, right sides together. Stitch on the marked line. Stitch again, ½" from the first line as shown. Cut between the two lines. Set aside the trimmed corner (see "Spare Triangle Square Ideas" on page 93). Press the seam

toward the light fabric. Repeat on the other end of the rectangle. Make 16.

Make 16.

3. Sew eight units into a row as shown. Press the seams in the direction shown. Make two rows.

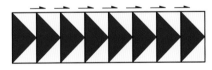

Make 2.

4. Sew the rows together as shown. Press the seam in either direction.

5. Refer to "Friendship Star Blocks" on page 15 to make four Friendship Star blocks from the leftover fabrics. You should now have 28 blocks for the border.

Flyby Mesh Tote

FINISHED TOTE SIZE: 21½" x 33½" (not including handles)

Materials

Yardages are based on 42"-wide fabrics.

- 6 fat quarters of assorted fabrics for flying-geese units
- ⅜ yard of focus fabric
- ⅜ yard of coordinating fabric for accent strips and insert cover
- 23" x 45" piece of nylon pet screen
- 3 yards of rickrack or decorative trim
- 1½ yards of eyelash fringe (optional)
- 6" x 22" piece of heavy cardboard for bag bottom

Cutting

From the assorted fat quarters, cut a *total* of:
- 16 pairs of squares (32 total), 3" x 3"
- 20 rectangles, 3" x 5½"*

From the coordinating fabric, cut:
- 4 strips, 1" x 23"
- 1 strip, 6" x 42"

From the focus fabric, cut:
- 2 strips, 4" x 23"

From the nylon pet screen, cut:
- 1 rectangle, 23" x 36"
- 2 strips, 3" x 23"

* To make the bag as shown, for each pair of squares cut a matching rectangle. You'll also need to cut 4 additional rectangles for a total of 20.

Constructing the Tote

1. Use a sharp pencil or fabric marking pen to draw a diagonal line from corner to corner on the wrong side of the fat-quarter squares.

2. Place a fat-quarter square on one end of a fat-quarter rectangle of a different fabric as shown, right sides together. Stitch on the marked line. Stitch again, ½" from the first stitching line as shown. Cut between the two lines. Set aside the trimmed corner for use in "Flyby Pouch," the bonus project on page 54, or for use in another project (refer to "Spare Triangle Square Ideas" on page 93). Press the seam toward the triangle. Repeat on the other end of the rectangle, using a square that matches the first square and positioning the square as shown, to complete the flying-geese unit. Make 16. You will have four fat-quarter rectangles left over.

3. Arrange eight flying-geese units into one horizontal strip as shown. To make the bag as shown, match the "goose" of each unit to the background fabric of the previous unit. Sew the units together. Press the seams in the direction shown. Sew a fat-quarter rectangle to each end of the strip. Trim the strip to 5½" x 23", keeping the flying-geese strip centered. Make two.

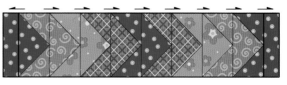

Make 2.

4. Fold the coordinating 1" x 23" strips in half lengthwise, wrong sides together. With the raw edges aligned, sew a strip to the long edge of each of the flying-geese strip units. Make sure the flying geese are pointing in the same direction on each strip or you will sew your coordinating strips to the wrong edges. Repeat to sew the remaining 1" x 23" coordinating strips to one long edge of each of the focus-fabric strips. Press the seams away from the coordinating strips.

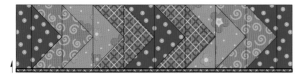

Make 2.

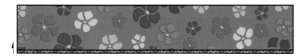

Make 2.

5. Pin the flying-geese units 7" from the ends of the nylon rectangle as shown. With right sides together, lay a focus-fabric strip on each flying-geese strip, aligning the raw edges of the focus-fabric and flying-geese strips. Sew ¼" from the raw edges of the strips, stitching through the nylon. Stitch close to the first seams to reinforce the stitching. Press the pieces open with a warm iron, being careful not to iron directly on the nylon so that it does not melt. Stitch in the ditch of the remaining seams.

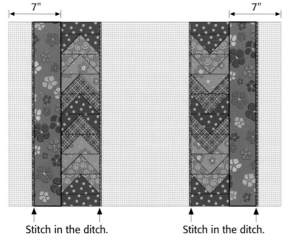

Stitch in the ditch. Stitch in the ditch.

6. Fold the bag piece in half, wrong sides together, matching the seams on the sides. Sew ¼" from the sides. Sew again, ⅛" from the sides, for reinforcement.

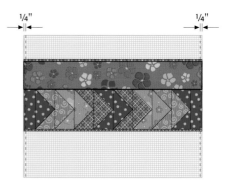

Turn the bag inside out. Sew ½" from the sides, enclosing the previous seams. Sew again, ⅜" from the sides for reinforcement.

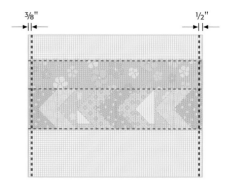

7. Flatten out one bottom corner of the bag as shown. Sew across the corner 2½" to 3" from the point. Sew again ¼" from the first stitching for reinforcement. Repeat on the opposite corner. Turn the bag right side out.

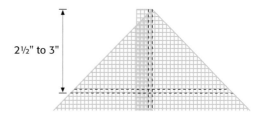

8. Fold the long edges of each nylon 3" x 23" strip toward the center of the strip, overlapping the edges to make a piece that is approximately 1¼" wide. Stitch through the center of each strip. Sew the rickrack or decorative trim over the nylon raw edges.

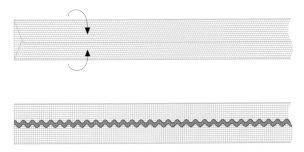

9. With the raw edges aligned and the wrong side facing up, place a strip from step 8 on the front of the bag, positioning the ends 5" from the sides as shown. Sew ¼" from the strip ends. Repeat to attach a strip to the back of the bag.

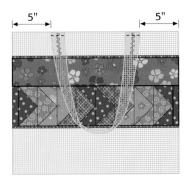

10. Fold the handles up, turn under the top raw edge ¾", and stitch the edge in place. If desired, add rickrack and eyelash trim to the top section of the bag.

11. To support the bottom, measure the length and width of the bag bottom. Cut two pieces of cardboard ½" smaller than the measurements. For example, the bottom should measure approximately 5½" x 21½", so you would cut two 5" x 20" pieces.

12. To make a cover for the cardboard pieces, fold the 6" x 42" coordinating fabric strip in half crosswise, right sides together. Sew along the long edges, leaving the short end open. Turn the cover right side out. Stack the cardboard pieces on top of each other and slip them into the open end of the cover. Tuck the excess fabric into the open end. Place the support into the bottom of the bag.

Flyby Pouch

1. Press open all the spare triangle squares you saved from "Flyby Mesh Tote." You should have 32.

2. Measure the triangle squares and trim them all to the size of the smallest one.

3. Stitch the triangle squares together to make a square or rectangular shape. Short and squat or long and narrow, the choice is yours. Refer to "Finishing Techniques" on page 89 to layer the piece with batting and backing; baste the layers together. Quilt in the ditch of each seam.

4. Measure the quilted piece and cut a piece of nylon pet screen the same size. Cut across the nylon piece in the direction you wish a zipper to run. Lay a zipper that is as long or longer than the cut edge between the two pieces. Place the edge of each nylon piece on opposite sides of the zipper teeth and topstitch in place.

The nylon will not ravel so there is no need to finish the edges. Make sure the zipper opens and closes.

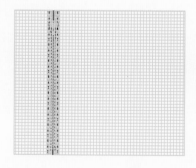

5. Lay the nylon piece and the quilted piece wrong sides together. Trim them to the same size if needed. Stitch all the way around the pieces using a ⅛" seam allowance.

6. Bind the pouch edges with a 2½"-wide strip of fabric. Add any trims or decorative features you wish.

Appliqué Star Blocks

FINISHED BLOCK SIZE: 6½" x 6½"

Materials

Yardages are based on 42"-wide fabrics. Materials listed are enough to make 10 blocks.

- ⅜ yard of fabric for stars
- ⅜ yard of fabric for background
- ½ yard of lightweight paper-backed fusible transfer web

Cutting

All measurements include ¼"-wide seam allowances.

From the background fabric, cut:
- 2 strips, 6½" x 42"; crosscut the strips into 10 squares, 6½" x 6½"

Appliquéing the Blocks

1. Trace the star pattern on page 56 onto the paper side of the transfer web 10 times, leaving a small amount of space between each motif. Follow the manufacturer's instructions to fuse the transfer web to the wrong side of the star fabric. Cut out the stars on the traced lines. Remove the paper backing.

2. Center and fuse each star to the right side of a 6½" background square.

3. Machine stitch around the edges of each star, using either a blanket stitch, zigzag stitch, feather stitch, or satin stitch. This will secure the appliqués to the fabric and prevent the edges from fraying.

NOTE: *This month you get a break from the Friendship Star blocks! Yippee! Of course, you could work ahead and get a few extra done just for the fun of it. Or, more likely, use the extra time from this easy month to catch up on the blocks you haven't made yet!*

Star

Happy Birthday Banner

FINISHED BANNER SIZE: 24½" x 42½" (not including hanging loops)

Materials

Yardages are based on 42"-wide fabrics.

- 9 fat quarters of assorted '30s prints OR ¾ yard *total* of assorted scraps for triangle squares, letters, stars, cake stand, and icing
- ¼ yard *each* of 6 light fabrics
- 1 fat quarter of fabric for cake
- 1½ yards of fabric for backing
- ⅜ yard of fabric for binding
- 29" x 47" piece of batting
- 1⅜ yards of jumbo rickrack for hanging loops
- 1 yard of small or medium rickrack for icing
- 1 yard *each* of 6 assorted colors of narrow (⅛"- to ⅜"-wide) grosgrain or double-faced satin ribbon
- ¼ yard of lightweight paper-backed fusible transfer web
- 13 assorted buttons for embellishment

Cutting

All measurements include ¼"-wide seam allowances.

From the 6 light fabrics, cut a *total* of:
- 3 squares, 4⅞" x 4⅞"; cut each square in half once diagonally to yield 6 triangles
- 2 rectangles, 4½" x 18½"
- 2 rectangles, 4½" x 22½"
- 2 rectangles, 4½" x 26½"

From *each* of the 9 fat quarters, cut:
- 2 squares, 4⅞" x 4⅞"; cut each square in half once diagonally to yield 36 triangles

From the cake fat quarter, cut:
- 1 rectangle, 4" x 6"
- 1 rectangle, 6" x 8"

From the binding fabric, cut:
- 4 strips, 2½" x 42"

Assembling the Banner Top

1. Sew each light triangle to a fat-quarter triangle to make a triangle square. Make six. Press the seams toward the fat-quarter triangles. Trim the dog-ears. The triangle squares should measure 4½" x 4½".

Make 6.

2. Sew one of the remaining fat-quarter triangles to a different fat-quarter triangle to make a triangle square. Make 12. Press the seams toward the darker triangle. Trim the dog-ears. The triangle squares should measure 4½" x 4½".

Make 12.

3. Sew one triangle square from step 1, two triangle squares from step 2, and one of the remaining fat-quarter triangles into vertical rows as shown. Make three of each row, paying careful attention to the placement of the light triangles. Press the seams toward the end triangles.

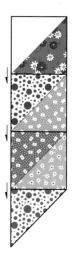

Make 3.   Make 3.

4. Arrange the light rectangles and the triangle-square rows as shown. Rearrange as necessary until you get a pleasing combination. Sew the light rectangles to the top of each triangle-square row. Press the seams toward the rectangles. Sew the rows together along the long edges. Press the seams away from the center.

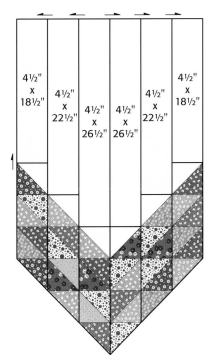

Appliquéing the Banner

1. Using the appliqué patterns on pages 60–63, trace the following shapes onto the paper side of the transfer web: five stars; one *each* of the cake plate, cake plate base, large icing, and small icing; and the letters needed to spell "Happy Birthday." Leave a small amount of space between each shape. Cut out each shape slightly beyond the traced lines. Follow the manufacturer's instructions to fuse the shapes to the wrong side of the remaining fat-quarter fabrics. Be sure to fuse the cake plate and base shapes to the same fabric and the large and small icing shapes to the same fabric. Cut out the appliqués on the traced lines. Remove the paper backing.

2. Refer to the photo on page 57 as needed to position the appliqués on the right side of the banner top. Follow the manufacturer's instructions to fuse the appliqués in place.

3. Using thread that matches the appliqué, machine stitch around the edges of each appliqué. Use either a blanket stitch, zigzag stitch, feather stitch, or satin stitch. This will secure the appliqués to the fabric and prevent the edges from fraying.

TIMESAVING IDEA!
Blanket stitching is usually done before the quilt top is layered and quilted. On smaller projects, I like to blanket-stitch around the appliqué pieces after the quilt is basted, going through all layers. It makes trying to figure out how to quilt around appliqués very easy—it's already done! It saves time, it has a nice look to it, and there are no quilting lines over the appliqué pieces.

Finishing the Banner

Refer to "Finishing Techniques" on page 89.

1. Trim the backing fabric so that it is approximately 4" longer and 4" wider than the quilt top.

2. Layer the quilt top with batting and backing; baste the layers together.

3. Quilt as desired. The appliquéd section of this banner was free-motion quilted with an allover small-loop design in the background. The appliqués were outline stitched to prevent them from becoming puffy. The triangle squares were stitched in the ditch.

4. Bind the banner with the 2½"-wide binding strips.

5. Cut the small or medium rickrack into two 6" lengths and two 8" lengths. Referring to the photo on page 57 for placement, use a straight stitch to sew the 6" lengths to the small cake section and the 8" lengths to the large cake section.

6. Wet the 1-yard lengths of grosgrain or satin ribbon and wrap each one around the handle of a wooden spoon, curlicue style. Let the ribbons air-dry or bake them in a 200° oven for one hour. Remove the ribbons from the spoons. Attach each ribbon to the banner front where desired by sewing a button through the center of each length.

STAYING POWER
Add a little starch to the ribbons when they are wet to make them stiffer.

7. Cut the jumbo rickrack into seven 6" lengths. Fold each length in half to make a loop. Stitch the ends of the loops to the back of the banner along the top bound edge, positioning a loop at each end and at each seam line. Stitch a button to the binding on the banner front at the base of each loop.

8. Add a label to the back of your project.

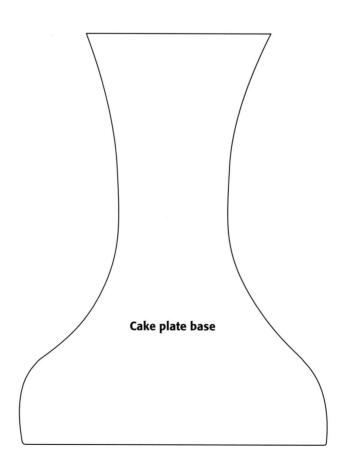

Cake plate base

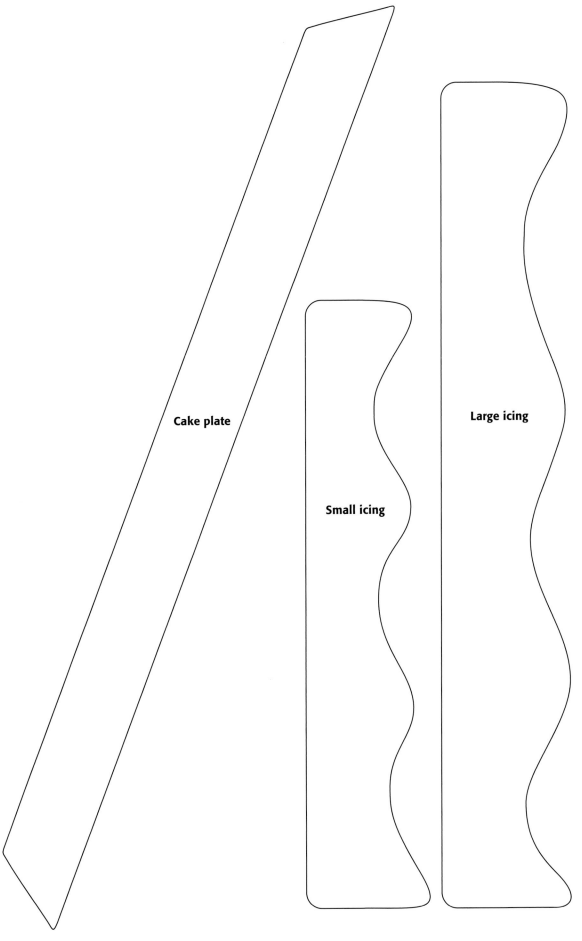

Cake plate

Small icing

Large icing

Supernova Blocks

FINISHED BLOCK SIZE: 10" x 10"

Materials

Yardages are based on 42"-wide fabrics. Materials listed are enough to make 4 blocks.

- ⅝ yard of light-colored fabric for block backgrounds and center star
- ⅜ yard of dark-colored fabric for outer star points
- ¼ yard of accent fabric for middle star points

Cutting

All measurements include ¼"-wide seam allowances.

From the light-colored fabric, cut:

- 3 strips, 2½" x 42"; crosscut the strips into 36 squares, 2½" x 2½"
- 2 strips, 1½" x 42"; crosscut the strips into 32 squares, 1½" x 1½"
- 2 strips, 2⅞" x 42"; crosscut the strips into 16 squares, 2⅞" x 2⅞". Cut each square in half once diagonally to yield 32 triangles.

From the dark-colored fabric, cut:

- 1 strip, 2½" x 42"; crosscut the strip into 16 squares, 2½" x 2½"
- 2 strips, 2⅞" x 42"; crosscut the strips into 16 squares, 2⅞" x 2⅞". Cut each square in half once diagonally to yield 32 triangles.

From the accent fabric, cut:

- 1 strip, 2½" x 42"; crosscut the strip into 16 squares, 2½" x 2½"
- 2 strips, 1½" x 42"; crosscut the strips into 32 squares, 1½" x 1½"

Piecing the Blocks

1. Sew a light triangle to each dark triangle to make a triangle square. Make 32. Press the seams toward the dark triangles. Trim the dog-ears. The triangle squares should measure 2½" x 2½".

Make 32.

2. Sew a triangle square to each dark 2½" square as shown. Make 16. Press the seam toward the dark square.

Make 16.

3. Sew the remaining triangle squares to each light 2½" square as shown. Make 16. Press the seam toward the light square.

Make 16.

4. Join the units from steps 2 and 3 as shown to make 16 outer-star-point units. Press the seams toward the dark-square units. The units should measure 4½" x 4½".

Make 16.

5. Use a sharp pencil or fabric marking pen to draw a diagonal line from corner to corner on the wrong side of the light and accent 1½" squares.

6. Place a light 1½" square on one corner of an accent 2½" square as shown, right sides together. Stitch on the marked line. Trim ¼" from the stitching line. Press the seam toward the triangle. Repeat on the opposite corner to complete an inner-star-point unit. Make 16.

Make 16.

7. Repeat step 6 with the accent 1½" squares and the light 2½" squares to make the middle-star-point units.

Make 16.

8. Sew each inner-star-point unit to a middle-star-point unit as shown. Make 16. Press the seams toward the inner-star-point units.

Make 16.

9. Sew a unit from step 8 to each side of a light 2½" square to make the block center row. Make four. Press the seams toward the square.

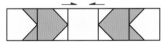

Make 4.

10. Join an outer-star-point unit from step 4 to each side of one of the remaining units from step 8. Make eight. Press the seams toward the outer-star-point units.

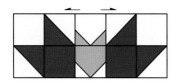

Make 8.

11. Sew a row from step 10 to the top and bottom edges of the center row from step 9 to complete the block. Make four. Press the seams toward the top and bottom rows. The blocks should measure 10½" x 10½".

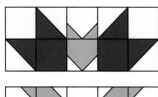

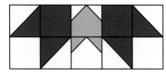

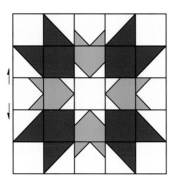

Make 4.

12. Sew the blocks into one horizontal row.

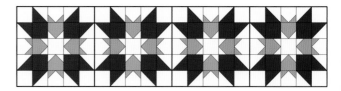

13. Refer to "Friendship Star Blocks" on page 15 to make four Friendship Star blocks from the leftover fabrics. You should now have 32 blocks for the border.

ENDLESS OPTIONS

The Supernova blocks are my favorite in the "Seeing Stars Quilt." It was hard to decide what the companion project using these blocks should be. Although I settled on a one-block table topper (shown on page 67), this block would also be great as the focus of a scrappy quilt. Just make all of your blocks with different-colored star and background fabrics. You could also make three matching blocks, sew them together side by side, and add a border to create a spectacular table runner. Combine these stars with sashing or set the blocks on point for even more options!

Supernova Table Topper

FINISHED TABLE TOPPER SIZE: 20" x 20"

Materials

Yardages are based on 42"-wide fabrics.

- ¼ yard of white fabric for block background and center star
- ¼ yard of navy blue fabric for middle star points
- ¼ yard of red fabric for outer star points
- ¼ yard of blue fabric for block border and outer corners
- ¼ yard of a different red fabric for accent corners
- ⅞ yard of fabric for backing
- 24" x 24" piece of batting

Cutting

All measurements include ¼"-wide seam allowances.

From the white fabric, cut:
- 9 squares, 2½" x 2½"
- 8 squares, 1½" x 1½"
- 4 squares, 2⅞" x 2⅞"; cut each square in half once diagonally to yield 8 triangles

From the red fabric for outer star points, cut:
- 4 squares, 2½" x 2½"
- 4 squares, 2⅞" x 2⅞"; cut each square in half once diagonally to yield 8 triangles

From the navy blue fabric, cut:
- 4 squares, 2½" x 2½"
- 8 squares, 1½" x 1½"

From the red fabric for accent corners, cut:
- 4 squares, 4½" x 4½"

From the blue fabric, cut:
- 2 squares, 7" x 7"; cut each square in half once diagonally to yield 4 triangles
- 2 rectangles, 2½" x 10½"
- 2 rectangles, 2½" x 14½"

Assembling the Table Topper Top

1. Sew a white triangle to each red triangle to make a triangle square. Make eight. Press the seams toward the red triangles. Trim the dog-ears. The triangle squares should measure 2½" x 2½".

Make 8.

2. Sew a triangle square to each red 2½" square as shown. Make four. Press the seams toward the red squares.

Make 4.

3. Sew one of the remaining triangle squares to a white 2½" square as shown. Make four. Press the seams toward the white squares.

Make 4.

4. Join the units from steps 2 and 3 as shown to make four outer-star-point units. Press the seams toward the red-square units. The units should measure 4½" x 4½".

Make 4.

5. Use a sharp pencil or fabric marking pen to draw a diagonal line from corner to corner on the wrong side of the white and navy blue 1½" squares.

6. Place a white 1½" square on one corner of a navy blue 2½" square as shown, right sides

together. Stitch on the marked line. Trim ¼"
from the stitching line. Press the seam toward
the triangle. Repeat on the opposite corner to
complete an inner-star-point unit. Make four.

Make 4.

7. Repeat step 6 with the navy blue 1½" squares
and the white 2½" squares to make the middle-
star-point units. Make four.

Make 4.

8. Sew each inner-star-point unit to a middle-
star-point unit as shown. Make four. Press the
seams toward the inner-star-point units.

Make 4.

9. Sew a unit from step 8 to each side of a white
2½" square to make the block center row.
Make one. Press the seams toward the square.

Make 1.

10. Join an outer-star-point unit from step 4 to
each side of one of the remaining units from
step 8 to make the block top row. Repeat to
make the block bottom row. Press the seams
toward the outer-star-point units.

Make 2.

11. Sew a row from step 10 to the top and bottom
edges of the center row from step 9 to complete the block. Press the seams toward the top
and bottom rows. The block should measure
10½" x 10½".

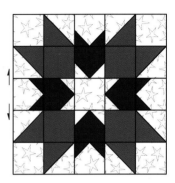

Make 1.

12. Sew the blue 2½" x 10½" rectangles to the
sides of the block. Press the seams toward the
rectangles. Sew the blue 2½" x 14½" rectangles to the top and bottom edges of the block.
Press the seams toward the rectangles. The
block should now measure 14½" x 14½".

13. Use a sharp pencil or fabric marking pen to draw a diagonal line from corner to corner on the wrong side of the red 4½" squares. Place a square on each corner of the block, positioning the square as shown. Stitch on the marked lines. Trim ¼" from the stitching lines. Press the seams toward the triangles.

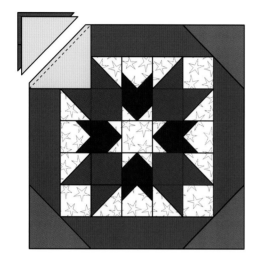

14. Center and sew a large blue triangle to all four sides of the block. Press the seams toward the blue triangles.

Finishing the Topper

Refer to "Finishing Techniques" on page 89.

1. Trim the batting so it is approximately 4" longer and 4" wider than the topper.

2. Lay the batting on a flat work surface. Place the backing, right side up, over the batting. Place the topper, wrong side up, over the backing. Use safety pins to pin-baste through all the layers.

3. Sew ¼" from the topper edges, leaving a 4" opening on one side of one of the blue triangles for turning. Sew over the seam again to reinforce it. Clip the corners and turn the topper to the right side. Push out all the corners using a wooden spoon or chopstick. Press carefully. You do not want any of your backing peeking around to the front. Slip-stitch the opening closed. Using a walking foot and matching thread colors, do some simple quilting in the ditch.

4. Add a label to the back of your project.

Holding Hands Star Blocks

FINISHED BLOCK SIZE: 10" x 6"

Materials

Yardages are based on 42"-wide fabrics. Materials listed are enough to make 2 blocks.

- ¼ yard of dark-colored fabric for background
- ¼ yard of medium-colored fabric for star
- ¼ yard of light-colored fabric for star

Cutting

All measurements include ¼"-wide seam allowances.

From the dark-colored fabric, cut:
- 2 strips, 2½" x 42"; crosscut the strips into:
  - 8 rectangles, 2½" x 4½"
  - 8 squares, 2½" x 2½"

From the medium-colored fabric, cut:
- 1 strip, 2½" x 42"; crosscut the strip into:
  - 2 rectangles, 2½" x 6½"
  - 4 squares, 2½" x 2½"

From the light-colored fabric, cut:
- 1 strip, 2½" x 42"; crosscut the strip into:
  - 2 rectangles, 2½" x 6½"
  - 4 squares, 2½" x 2½"

Piecing the Blocks

1. Use a sharp pencil or fabric marking pen to draw a diagonal line from corner to corner on the wrong side of all of the light and medium squares and four of the dark squares.

2. Place a medium square on one end of a dark 2½" x 4½" rectangle as shown. Stitch on the marked line. Stitch again, ½" from the first stitching line as shown. Cut between the two lines. Set aside the trimmed corner (see "Spare Triangle Square Ideas" on page 93). Press the seam toward the triangle. Make four. Repeat with the light squares and the dark rectangles.

Make 4.   Make 4.

3. Join the medium and light units from step 2 and the dark squares as shown to make the block top and bottom rows. Make two of each. Press the seams toward the dark squares.

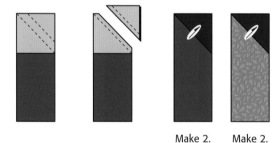

Top row.
Make 2.

Bottom row.
Make 2.

4. Place a dark square on one end of a medium 2½" x 6½" rectangle as shown. Stitch on the marked line. Stitch again, ½" from the first stitching line as shown. Cut between the two lines. Set aside the trimmed corner (see "Spare Triangle Square Ideas" on page 93). Press the seam toward the triangle. Make two. Repeat with the dark squares and the light rectangles.

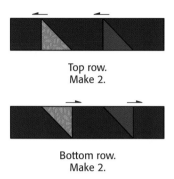

Make 2.   Make 2.

5. To make the block middle row, place a medium and light unit from step 4 right sides together as shown. Use a sharp pencil or fabric marking pen to draw a diagonal line from the lower left corner of the light rectangle to the upper right corner of the medium rectangle.

Stitch on the marked line. Stitch again, ½" from the first stitching line as shown. Cut between the two lines. Set aside the trimmed corner (see "Spare Triangle Square Ideas" on page 93). Press the seam in the direction shown. Make two.

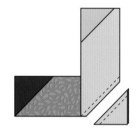

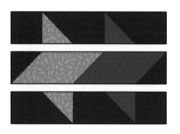

Make 2.

6. Join a top, middle, and bottom row together as shown to complete the block. Make two. Press the seams toward the middle rows. The blocks should measure 10½" x 6½".

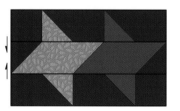

Make 2.

7. Refer to "Friendship Star Blocks" on page 15 to make four Friendship Star blocks with the leftover fabrics. You should now have a total of 36 blocks.

Holding Hands Place Mats and Napkins

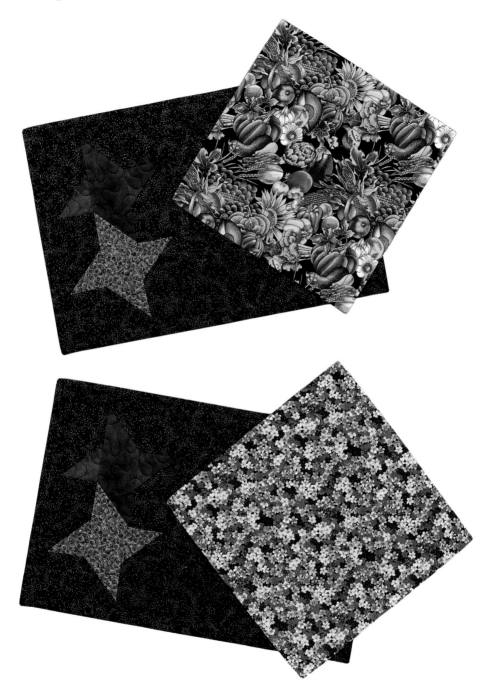

FINISHED PLACE MAT SIZE: 18¾" x 12"
FINISHED NAPKIN SIZE: 12" x 12"

Materials

Yardages are based on 42"-wide fabrics. Materials listed are enough for 6 place mats and 6 napkins.

- 2¼ yards of black fabric for star background, place mat body, and binding
- ⅞ yard of a coordinating multicolored print fabric for napkins
- ¼ yard of red fabric for star
- ¼ yard of green fabric for star
- 1⅛ yards of fabric for backing
- 1⅛ yards of batting
- Decorative thread for napkins
- Template plastic or lightweight cardboard

Cutting

All measurements include ¼"-wide seam allowances.

From the black fabric, cut:

- 2 strips, 11½" x 42"; crosscut the strips into 6 rectangles, 11½" x 12"
- 4 strips, 1¼" x 42"; crosscut the strips into:
  - 12 rectangles, 1¼" x 6½"
  - 6 rectangles, 1¼" x 12"
- 5 strips, 2½" x 42"; crosscut the strips into:
  - 24 rectangles, 2½" x 4½"
  - 24 squares, 2½" x 2½"
- 12 strips, 2½" x 42"

From the red fabric, cut:

- 2 strips, 2½" x 42"; crosscut the strips into:
  - 6 rectangles, 2½" x 6½"
  - 12 squares, 2½" x 2½"

From the green fabric, cut:

- 2 strips, 2½" x 42"; crosscut the strips into:
  - 6 rectangles, 2½" x 6½"
  - 12 squares, 2½" x 2½"

From the backing, cut:

- 6 rectangles, 14" x 20"

From the batting, cut:

- 6 rectangles, 14" x 20"

From the multicolored print, cut:

- 2 strips, 14" x 42"; crosscut the strips into 6 squares, 14" x 14"

SELECTING FABRICS

I purposely picked black fabric for these place mats because I didn't want to worry too much about spills. Any family with small children will find this a bonus feature. For the backing, I used a large-scale floral print so that the place mats would be reversible.

Assembling the Place Mat Tops

1. Use a sharp pencil or fabric marking pen to draw a diagonal line from corner to corner on the wrong side of all of the green and red squares and 12 of the black squares.

2. Place a green square on one end of a black 2½" x 4½" rectangle as shown. Stitch on the marked line. Stitch again, ½" from the first stitching line as shown. Cut between the two lines. Set aside the trimmed corner (see "Spare Triangle Square Ideas" on page 93). Press the seam toward the triangle. Make 12. Repeat with the red squares and the 2½" x 4½" black rectangles.

Make 12.   Make 12.

3. Join the red and green units from step 2 and the unmarked black squares as shown to make the block top and bottom rows. Make six of each. Press the seams toward the black squares.

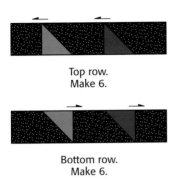

Top row.
Make 6.

Bottom row.
Make 6.

4. Place a black square on one end of a red 2½" x 6½" rectangle as shown. Stitch on the marked line. Stitch again, ½" from the first stitching line as shown. Cut between the two lines. Set aside the trimmed corner (see "Spare Triangle Square Ideas" on page 93). Press the seam toward the triangle. Make six. Repeat with the black squares and the green rectangles.

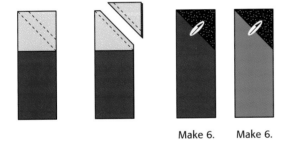

Make 6.   Make 6.

5. To make the block middle row, place a green and a red unit from step 4 right sides together as shown. Use a sharp pencil or fabric marking pen to draw a diagonal line from the lower left corner of the green rectangle to the upper right corner of the red rectangle. Stitch on the marked line. Stitch again, ½" from the first stitching line as shown. Cut between the two

lines. Set aside the trimmed corner (see "Spare Triangle Square Ideas" on page 93). Press the seam in the direction shown. Make two.

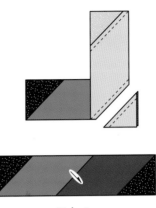

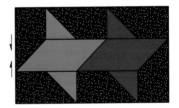

Make 2.

6. Join a top, middle, and bottom row together as shown to complete the block. Make six. Press the seams toward the middle rows. The blocks should measure 10½" x 6½".

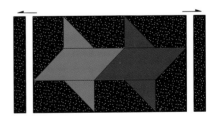

Make 6.

7. Sew a black 1¼" x 6½" rectangle to the sides of each block as shown. Press the seams toward the rectangles.

8. Sew a black 1¼" x 12" rectangle to the top of each block. Make sure all of the blocks are oriented the same. Press the seams toward the rectangle.

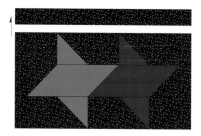

9. Join a black 11½" x 12" rectangle to each block as shown to complete the place mat top. Press the seams toward the place mat body. The place mats should measure 18¾" x 12".

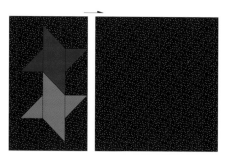

Finishing the Place Mats

Refer to "Finishing Techniques" on page 89.

1. Layer each place mat top with batting and backing; baste the layers together.

2. Quilt as desired. These place mats were free-motion quilted with an allover design.

3. Bind the edges of each place mat with the black 2½"-wide strips.

Making the Napkins

1. Turn under each side of each 14" multicolored print square ¼" to the wrong side. Use matching thread to stitch the edge in place. This hem doesn't have to look neat on the corners yet. Just fold it under and stitch it in place.

2. Trace the trimming pattern at the bottom of the page onto template plastic or cardboard. With right sides together, fold each hemmed square in half diagonally. Lay the triangle template on opposite corners of the folded square as shown and use a sharp pencil to mark the template edge that faces the inside of the square. Stitch on the marked lines, stitching completely across the points of the square. Trim ¼" from the stitching lines. Refold the square on the opposite diagonal and repeat to stitch and trim the remaining two corners.

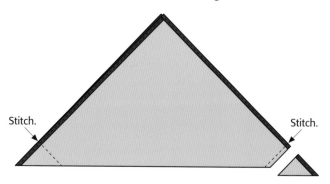

Stitch.　　　　　Stitch.

3. Turn the corners out and press the squares. This creates mitered corners on the wrong side. Using decorative thread, topstitch close to the hemmed edge.

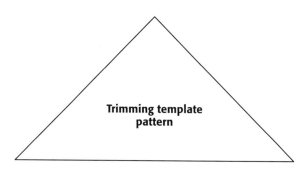

Trimming template pattern

Comet Tail Blocks

FINISHED BLOCK SIZE: 10" x 10"

Materials

Yardages are based on 42"-wide fabrics. Materials listed are enough to make 2 blocks.

- ⅜ yard of light-colored fabric
- ⅜ yard of dark-colored fabric

Cutting

All measurements include ¼"-wide seam allowances.

From the light-colored fabric, cut:

- 1 strip, 4½" x 42"; crosscut the strip into 8 squares, 4½" x 4½"
- 1 strip, 2½" x 42"; crosscut the strip into:
  - 2 rectangles, 2½" x 10½"
  - 2 squares, 2½" x 2½"
- 4 squares, 1½" x 1½"

From the dark-colored fabric, cut:

- 1 strip, 4½" x 42"; crosscut the strip into 8 squares, 4½" x 4½"
- 1 strip, 2½" x 42"; crosscut the strip into:
  - 2 rectangles, 2½" x 4½"
  - 6 squares, 2½" x 2½"

Piecing the Blocks

1. Use a sharp pencil or fabric marking pen to draw a line from corner to corner on the wrong side of the light 4½" and 1½" squares, and four of the dark 2½" squares.

2. Place a light and dark 4½" square right sides together with the light square on top. Stitch on the marked line. Stitch again, ½" from the first stitching line as shown. Cut between the two

lines. Set aside the trimmed corner (see "Spare Triangle Square Ideas" on page 93). Press the seam toward the dark triangle. Make eight.

Make 8.

3. Sew two triangle-square units together as shown to make mirror-image pairs. Make two of each pair. Press the seams in the direction indicated.

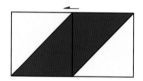

Make 2.   Make 2.

4. Place a light 1½" square on one corner of an unmarked dark 2½" square as shown. Stitch on the marked line. Trim ¼" from the stitching line. Press the seam toward the triangle. Repeat on the opposite corner. Make two.

Make 2.

5. Join the units from step 4, a light 2½" square, and a dark 2½" x 4½" rectangle as shown. Make two. Press the seams toward the rectangle.

Make 2.

6. Sew one of the triangle-square pairs from step 3 to the sides of the unit from step 5 as shown.

Make two. Press the seams toward the step 3 units.

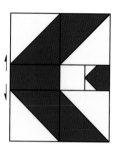

Make 2.

7. Place a dark 2½" square on one end of a light 2½" x 10½" rectangle, right sides together. Stitch on the marked line. Stitch again, ½" from the first stitching line as shown. Cut between the two lines. Set aside the trimmed corner (see "Spare Triangle Square Ideas" on page 93). Press the seam toward the dark triangle. Repeat on the opposite end of the rectangle, positioning the square as shown. Make two.

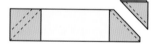

Make 2.

8. Join one unit each from steps 6 and 7 as shown to complete the block. Make two. Press the seams toward the step 7 unit. The blocks should measure 10½" x 10½".

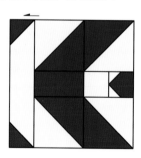

Make 2.

9. Refer to "Friendship Star Blocks" on page 15 to make your last four Friendship Star blocks from the leftover fabrics. You should have a total of 40 blocks for the border.

Pillowcase

Finished pillowcase size: 20" x 27" (standard size)

Materials

Yardages are based on 42"-wide fabrics.

- ¾ yard of fabric for pillowcase body
- ½ yard of fabric for accent

Cutting

All measurements include ¼"-wide seam allowances.

From the pillowcase body fabric, cut:
- 1 rectangle, 22½" x 42"

From the accent fabric, cut:
- 1 rectangle, 15" x 42"

Making the Pillowcase

1. With *wrong* sides together, sew the accent rectangle to the body rectangle along the long edge, using a ¼" seam allowance. From the wrong side, press the seam toward the accent fabric. Fold the fabric *right* sides together along the seam line. Stitch ½" from the sewn edge to encase the previous seam. From the right side, press the seam to one side. This finished seam is called a French seam. It is perfect for a pillowcase because there are no exposed edges.

2. Fold the pillowcase in half crosswise, wrong sides together. Sew ¼" from the edges as shown in the illustration. Press the seam to one side. Turn the pillowcase to the wrong side so the right sides are together. Stitch ½" from the sewn edges to encase the previous seam. Press.

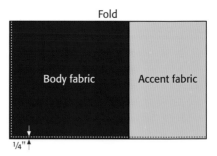

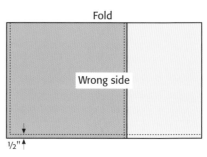

3. Fold the accent fabric ¼" to the wrong side and stitch it in place. Fold the accent fabric again so that the hemmed edge just covers the French seam.

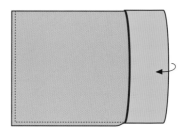

4. Turn the body portion of the pillowcase right side out. Stitch the hemmed accent edge to the French seam. Press.

Zigzag Strip

FINISHED STRIP SIZE: 4" x 56"

Materials

Yardages are based on 42"-wide fabrics. Materials listed are enough for 2 strips.

- ⅜ yard of dark-colored fabric
- ⅜ yard of light-colored fabric

Cutting

All measurements include ¼"-wide seam allowances.

From the dark-colored fabric, cut:

- 3 squares, 9¼" x 9¼"; cut each square in half twice diagonally to yield 12 large triangles

From the light-colored fabric, cut:

- 4 squares, 9¼" x 9¼"; cut each square in half twice diagonally to yield 16 large triangles. You will use 14 and have 2 left over.
- 2 squares, 4⅞" x 4⅞"; cut each square in half once diagonally to yield 4 small triangles

Piecing the Strips

1. Stitch six large dark triangles and seven large light triangles together as shown. You will be stitching bias edges together so treat them gently, and do not pull on these at all! Be very careful to guide the pieces through the machine with a light touch. Make two strips.

Make 2.

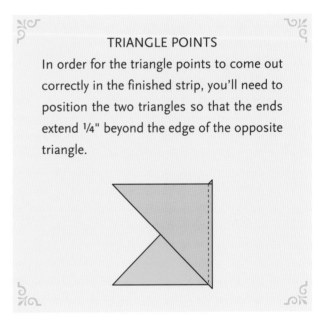

TRIANGLE POINTS

In order for the triangle points to come out correctly in the finished strip, you'll need to position the two triangles so that the ends extend ¼" beyond the edge of the opposite triangle.

2. Sew a small light triangle to each end of the strips as shown.

Zigzag Crib Quilt

FINISHED QUILT SIZE: 48" x 60"

Materials

Yardages are based on 42"-wide fabrics.

- 10 fat quarters of assorted pink and purple fabrics
- 2½ yards of light-colored fabric for background, border, and binding
- 3 yards of fabric for backing
- 54" x 66" piece of batting

Cutting

All measurements include ¼"-wide seam allowances.

From the light-colored fabric, cut:

- 15 squares, 9¼" x 9¼"; cut each square in half twice diagonally to yield 60 triangles
- 6 strips, 5" x 42"
- 6 strips, 2½" x 42"

From *each* of the 10 fat quarters, cut:

- 2 squares, 9¼" x 9¼"; cut each square in half twice diagonally to yield 8 triangles. You will use 7 and have 1 left over.
- 1 square, 4⅞" x 4⅞"; cut each square in half once diagonally to yield 2 triangles

Assembling the Quilt Top

1. Stitch six light triangles and seven of the large, same-color fat-quarter triangles together as shown. You will be stitching bias edges together so treat them gently, and do not pull on these at all! Be very careful to guide the pieces through the machine with a light touch. Make 10 strips.

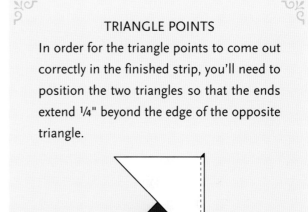

Make 10 total.

TRIANGLE POINTS

In order for the triangle points to come out correctly in the finished strip, you'll need to position the two triangles so that the ends extend ¼" beyond the edge of the opposite triangle.

2. Sew a small fat-quarter triangle that is the same color as the strip triangles to the ends of each strip as shown.

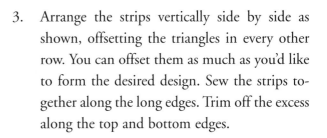

3. Arrange the strips vertically side by side as shown, offsetting the triangles in every other row. You can offset them as much as you'd like to form the desired design. Sew the strips together along the long edges. Trim off the excess along the top and bottom edges.

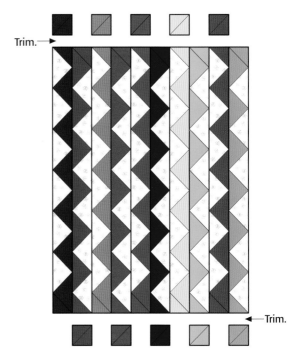

Trim.

Trim.

4. Refer to "Adding Borders" on page 89 to measure the quilt top for the top and bottom borders. Cut two of the light 5" x 42" strips to the length measured. Sew the strips to the top and bottom edges of the quilt top. Press the seams toward the border strips. Measure the quilt top for the side borders. Join the remaining light-colored 5" x 42" strips end to end to make one long strip. From the pieced strip, cut two strips to the length measured. Sew the strips to the sides of the quilt top. Press the seams toward the border strips.

Finishing the Quilt

Refer to "Finishing Techniques" on page 89.

1. Piece the quilt backing so that it is approximately 6" longer and 6" wider than the quilt top.

2. Layer the quilt top, batting, and backing; baste the layers together.

3. Quilt as desired. This quilt was quilted with white thread and a stippling design in the white areas. The pink areas were free-motion quilted with swirly circles and pink thread. The purple areas were straight-line quilted with purple thread.

4. Bind the quilt with the light 2½"-wide binding strips.

5. Add a label to the back of your project.

Seeing Stars Quilt Construction

FINISHED QUILT SIZE: 84½" x 104½"

Materials

Yardages are based on 42"-wide fabrics. You will need the following materials in addition to the blocks you constructed in the previous months and the zigzag strips you constructed this month.

- 1 yard of light-colored fabric for spacer strips
- 1½ yards of medium- to dark-colored fabric for outer border
- 8 yards of fabric for backing
- ⅞ yard of fabric for binding
- 92" x 111" piece of batting

Cutting

All measurements include ¼"-wide seam allowances.

From the light-colored fabric, cut:

- 8 strips, 2½" x 42"

From the medium- to dark-colored fabric, cut:

- 10 strips, 4½" x 42"

From the binding fabric, cut:

- 10 strips, 2½" x 42"

Assembling the Quilt Top

1. Sew together two Chain Star blocks from month three and one Spacey Star block from month five as shown. Make four. Be sure the blocks are oriented the same in each group.

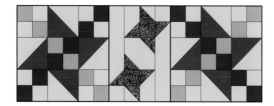

Make 4.

2. Sew a unit from step 1 to the sides of the center star unit from month two. Join an Evening Star block from month four to the ends of the two remaining units. Sew these units to the top and bottom edges of the center star unit. The center unit should now measure 56½" x 56½".

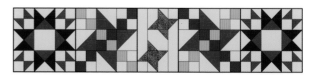

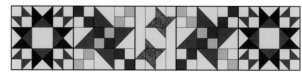

3. Attach a zigzag strip from month twelve to the sides of the unit from step 2 as shown.

4. Sew two Mosaic Star blocks from month six to each side of the Geese in the Stars block from month seven as shown. Attach a Comet Tail block from month eleven to the ends of the Supernova strip from month nine as shown. These units should measure 10½" x 60½".

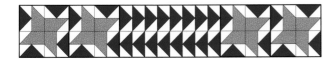

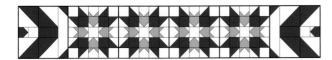

5. Join the light 2½"-wide strips together end to end to make one long strip. From the pieced strip, cut four 60½"-long strips and four 14½"-long strips. Sew the 60½"-long strips to both long edges of the block units from step 4. Sew the 14½"-long strips to the short ends of the units.

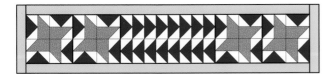

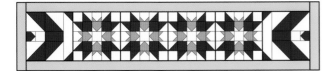

6. Attach the Supernova strip to the top edge of the quilt top. Join the Mosaic Star unit to the bottom edge of the quilt top.

7. Arrange seven Friendship Star blocks, two Appliqué Star blocks from month eight, and one Holding Hands Star block from month ten as desired into a horizontal strip for the top and bottom borders. Make two. Stitch the strips to the top and bottom of the quilt top. Arrange 13 Friendship Star blocks and three Appliqué Star blocks as desired to make the side borders. Make two. Sew the strips to the sides of the quilt top.

8. Sew the 4½"-wide outer-border strips together end to end to make one long strip. Refer to "Adding Borders" on page 89 to measure the quilt top for the top and bottom borders. From the pieced strip, cut two strips to the length measured. Sew the strips to the top and bottom edges of the quilt top. Press the seams toward the border strips. Measure the quilt top for the side borders. From the remainder of the pieced strip, cut two strips to the length measured. Sew the strips to the sides of the quilt top. Press the seams toward the border strips.

Finishing the Quilt

Refer to "Finishing Techniques" on page 89.

1. Piece the quilt backing so that it is approximately 6" longer and 6" wider than the quilt top.

2. Layer the quilt top, batting, and backing; baste the layers together.

3. Quilt as desired. I highly recommend machine quilting a top of this size with an allover stippling or loop design.

4. Bind the quilt with the 2½"-wide binding strips.

5. Add a label to the back of your project.

Finishing Techniques

Don't stop once the top is done! Enjoy your quilt by referring to this section to finish it up.

Adding Borders

With the exception of "Pinwheel Piggies Baby Quilt" on page 20, all of the quilts in this book have borders with straight-cut corners. The cutting instructions will indicate the number of strips to cut across the width of the fabric. If you are working on a large quilt with sides that are longer than the width of the fabric, you will need to piece the strips together end to end and then cut the pieced strip to the exact length. Use a diagonal seam when piecing the strips together to eliminate bulk. Press the seam open.

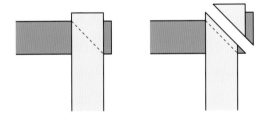

Joining straight-grain strips

I always measure my quilt top before I cut the border pieces. This is a wise decision in case you need to adjust border lengths. I usually measure the width of the quilt first by taking the measurements at the top and bottom edges and through the horizontal center. Ideally these measurements will all be the same. If they are not, I will average the length and cut two border strips the same length. After I add these strips to the top and bottom, I measure the sides at both edges and through the vertical center. The same principal applies here; the measurements should all be the same, but if not, average and cut both border strips the same length. Attach these strips to the sides of the quilt top. Press the seam allowances toward the border strips after each addition.

Pinning the border strips to the quilt top also makes a huge difference. If you pin before you sew, the borders will shift or migrate less and will stay where you want them. For the best results, never sew a strip of fabric on and trim the extra fabric when you get to the end. That is how quilt edges develop ripples and a distorted shape. The quilt will be squarer and lie flatter if you measure, cut, pin, and then sew.

Layering and Basting

The quilt "sandwich" includes three layers: the backing, batting, and quilt top. Prepare the backing so that it is several inches larger than the quilt top on all sides. For larger quilts, allow at least 3" on each side; smaller projects can get by with about 2" extra on each side. Cut your batting the same size as the backing.

Lay the backing wrong side up on a clean, flat surface. Secure it with masking tape or binder clips, making sure it is taut but not stretched out of shape. Position the batting over the backing and smooth it out. Center the quilt top over the batting, right side up. Baste the layers together. For hand quilting, thread baste a diagonal line from corner to corner and then add vertical rows spaced no more than 6" apart. For machine quilting, baste the layers with No. 2 rustproof safety pins placed 3" to 4" apart.

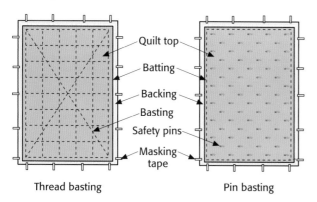

Thread basting   Pin basting

Quilting

"QUILT AS DESIRED." These famous words can be found at the end of nearly every quilt pattern and often leave beginner and sometimes even experienced quilters wanting more. Hand quilting is a wonderful way to finish off quilt tops but it is also a very time-consuming process. If you have the time and commitment for this method, the effects are lovely.

Machine quilting is my quilting method of choice. I enjoy the look, speed, and durability of the process. I own a long-arm quilting machine and appreciate the fact that I can easily finish my larger quilts on it. I usually quilt them with an allover pattern such as stippling or wandering loops. A local quilt shop may have machine quilting available to you or know of someone who can quilt for you. It is worth the expense of getting it machine quilted to not have to struggle with the size and weight of a large quilt while trying to do it on your home sewing machine.

Smaller projects, however, can easily be quilted on a home sewing machine. Use either a walking foot for stitching in the ditch and for straight lines, or a darning foot with the feed dogs disengaged for free-motion quilting. Quilt shops often offer classes to guide you through the basics of machine quilting and will stock tools and notions to make this task easier. The single most important thing to keep in mind with machine quilting is that it takes practice, practice, and more practice. Do not judge your future machine-quilting abilities on your first attempt. Take a class and keep on trying. Start with doodling on paper. When that becomes easy, move up to quilting on scrap fabric and batting "sandwiches." Practice every day for a while to get comfortable with the concept. There are lots of tools available to help you achieve success. And did I mention practice?

Binding

AFTER YOUR quilt is quilted, trim the backing and batting even with the quilt top. Now you are ready to bind the raw edges. The cutting instructions for each project will indicate the number of 2½"-wide strips to cut across the width of the fabric for the binding. If you like narrower binding, cut the strips 2¼" wide.

1. Sew the strips together end to end to make one long strip. Trim the seams to ¼" and press them open.

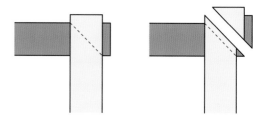

2. Fold the strip in half lengthwise, wrong sides together; press. (Some people, like me, skip the pressing but it does make a nice crisp edge to sew later on.)

3. Place the binding on the front of the quilt top near the center of one side. Align the raw edges of the binding with the raw edges of the quilt top. Using a walking foot, sew the binding to the quilt with a ¼" seam; leave the first 8" of the binding unstitched. Stop stitching ¼" from the corner, backstitch, and remove the quilt from the machine.

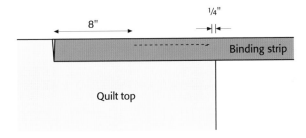

4. Fold the binding up at a 45° angle. Pin the binding at the edge and then fold the binding back down so that the raw edge is even with the next edge of the quilt. Begin stitching at the edge of the quilt and stop stitching ¼" from the next corner. Repeat the folding and stitching process at each corner.

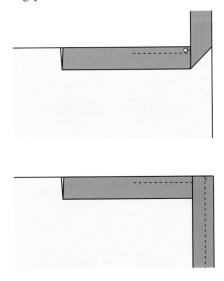

5. Stop sewing about 10" from where you began stitching; backstitch and remove the quilt from the machine. You'll have two overlapping tails and 10" of space. Lay the quilt on a flat surface and trim the tails so that they overlap

by exactly the width of the binding you are using. You can use your binding (opened up, not folded) as a measuring tool.

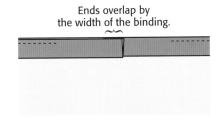

Ends overlap by the width of the binding.

6. Open up the ends. Place the ends right sides together as shown. Stitch diagonally from the top left corner of the top strip to the bottom right corner of the bottom strip. It is easier if you mark this line first and then pin the pieces together and stitch. *Before* you trim the seam to ¼", test to be sure you sewed it correctly and that it lies flat. Adjust as necessary. Now, isn't that nice! Finger-press the seam open.

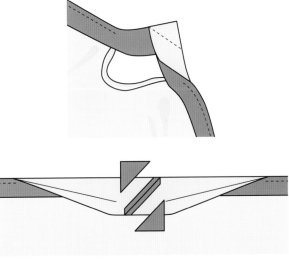

Press open and trim to ¼".

7. Refold the strip and sew the unstitched portion of the binding to the quilt, overlapping the previous lines of stitching.

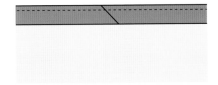

8. Fold the binding over the raw edge and slip-stitch or invisible stitch it by hand to the back of the quilt.

FINISH IT EVEN FASTER!

Alternatively, you could sew the binding to the *back* of the quilt, fold it over to the front, and topstitch the edges in place by machine from the front. You could even use some of those decorator stitches you have on your sewing machine! This method is really great for baby quilts, quilts that will get heavy use, and when you're tired of binding by hand!

Making a Label

ALL QUILTS should be labeled! You want future generations to know who made the quilt and the occasion that it celebrates. Labels also make it easier to identify the owner of the quilt if it is lost or stolen. Labels can be elaborate or simple. You can use a fabric pen on muslin to hand write the information, or you can even run fabric sheets through your computer printer and make labels right from your computer. There is no end to the possibilities! Just make sure it gets done. Be sure to include information such as the name of the maker and the quilter; the quilt pattern and designer; the date it was started and finished; the reason the quilt was made or the pattern was chosen; the occasion the quilt was made to celebrate; the owner's name, address, and telephone number; and how to care for the quilt. Below is a sample label for you to trace onto a light-colored fabric. Fill in the details, using acid-free permanent pens and markers.

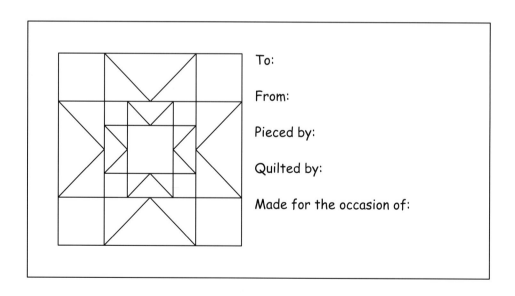

To:

From:

Pieced by:

Quilted by:

Made for the occasion of:

Spare Triangle Square Ideas

THE METHODS used to create blocks in this book simplify the piecing and create lots of extra triangle squares that you can use on other projects. I've included a few ideas as bonus projects and I wanted to show you a few more examples of what you can do with your spare blocks. There are no directions for these quilts. They are only shown as ideas for jump-starting your own creative process to make something wonderful out of leftovers.

For more ideas, peruse your collection of quilting books and look for blocks that use triangle squares in two or three colors. You will find many blocks in which to use up the spares. Sometimes you will be able to work these leftovers into scrappy patterns that call for triangle squares. Be on the lookout for opportunities in patterns and magazines.

If you want to be a little creative, break out the graph paper and make up your own block. Better yet, have a youngster design a block on graph paper and then make the quilt for them! There is no end to what you can make. Don't be afraid to try something new and different.

You can also challenge your quilting friends. Give each of them some of the leftover triangle squares and ask them to make a block for you. It will be interesting to see how they use the squares and what fabrics they combine them with.

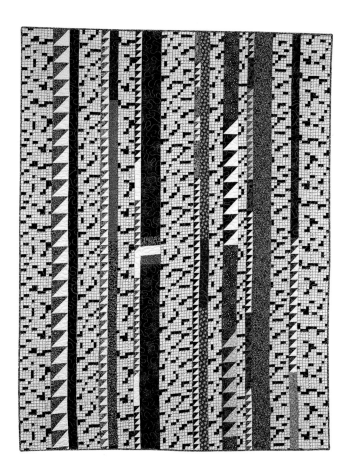

Vertical Stripes, 65¾" x 84¾"

I accumulated the spare triangles from the black-and-white version of "Seeing Stars Quilt" and combined them with leftover strips of fabric from the same quilt and a great crossword-puzzle print. It would be a lot of fun to fill in all those spaces with words! I had originally intended to put this on the back of "Seeing Stars Quilt" but when I finished it, I decided it really needed to be its very own quilt. I used up nearly every bit of leftover fabric from that project to make this quilt top. What a fantastic finish!

Horizontal Stripes, 55¼" x 91"

The bright "Seeing Stars Quilt" is my favorite of all the color combinations. Even friends who don't like these kinds of colors love this quilt more than the others. I intended it to be bold and bright and it is! Like "Vertical Stripes," these leftovers also were intended to go on the back of the bright "Seeing Stars Quilt" but when I got it done, it became a quilt of its own. I set the extra pieces apart with a bright border print that was cut up and almost unrecognizable from its original form. So many have claimed this quilt as the one they want. I just may have to keep it for myself.

Seeing Stars

16 Quilted Projects

Shelley Lynne Robson

Martingale®
& Company

CREDITS

President	*Nancy J. Martin*
CEO	*Daniel J. Martin*
VP and General Manager	*Tom Wierzbicki*
Publisher	*Jane Hamada*
Editorial Director	*Mary V. Green*
Managing Editor	*Tina Cook*
Technical Editor	*Laurie Baker*
Copy Editor	*Ellen Balstad*
Design Director	*Stan Green*
Illustrator	*Laurel Strand*
Cover Designer	*Regina Girard*
Text Designer	*Trina Craig*
Photographer	*Brent Kane*

That Patchwork Place® is an imprint of
Martingale & Company®.

Seeing Stars: 16 Quilted Projects
© 2005 by Shelley Lynne Robson

Martingale & Company
20205 144th Avenue NE
Woodinville, WA 98072-8478 USA
www.martingale-pub.com

Printed in China
10 09 08 07 06 05   8 7 6 5 4 3 2 1

Library of Congress Cataloging-in-Publication Data

Robson, Shelley Lynne.
    Seeing stars : 16 quilted projects / Shelley Lynne Robson.
        p. cm.
    ISBN 1-56477-630-1
    1. Patchwork—Patterns. 2. Quilting. 3. Star quilts. I. Title.
    TT835.R6216 2005
    746.46'041—dc22

                                                    2005012746

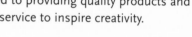

MISSION STATEMENT

Dedicated to providing quality products and
service to inspire creativity.